FROM Puppy TO PERFECT

For my father, who has never consulted the instructions

A SIMPLE STEP-BY-STEP TRAINING GUIDE

Including a lesson from Ian and Wendy Openshaw on placeboard training

FROM Puppy TO PERFECT

A PROVEN, PRACTICAL GUIDE TO TRAINING AND CARING FOR YOUR NEW PUPPY

JANET MENZIES

Quiller

CONTENTS

Copyright © 2015 Janet Menzies

First published in the UK in 2015 by Quiller, an imprint of Quiller Publishing Ltd

British Library Cataloguing-in-Publication Data
A catalogue record for this book is available from the British Library

ISBN 978 1 84689 205 9

The right of Janet Menzies to be identified as the author of this work has been asserted in accordance with the Copyright, Design and Patent Act 1988

The information in this book is true and complete to the best of our knowledge. All recommendations are made without any guarantee on the part of the Publisher, who also disclaims any liability incurred in connection with the use of this data or specific details.

All rights reserved. No part of this book may be reproduced or transmitted in any form or by any means, electronic or mechanical including photocopying, recording or by any information storage and retrieval system, without permission from the Publisher in writing.

Book and cover design by Sharyn Troughton
Printed in China

Quiller

An imprint of Quiller Publishing Ltd
Wykey House, Wykey, Shrewsbury, SY4 1JA
Tel: 01939 261616 Fax: 01939 261606
E-mail: info@quillerbooks.com
Website: www.quillerpublishing.com

ACKNOWLEDGEMENTS

Whenever I am writing about dogs and training, I am struck by how much there is to know about training dogs. Luckily for me, I have many friends who know a great deal about dog training, and are always extremely generous not only with their knowledge but also their time and support. Ian and Wendy Openshaw contributed the section on placeboard training, and it is an honour to be able to include these two trainers I admire so much in the book. Another top spaniel trainer and Kennel Club committee member, Jon Bailey, and his wife, Catherine, are currently helping me with FTCh Gournaycourt Ginger, and his daughter Fernmoss Gold Dust of Gournaycourt (who appears in this book under the rather more yellable name of Fizz) and we all have our fingers crossed for future competitions. Roy and Sandra Ellershaw, who bred Fizz, somehow managed to complete her training before passing her on to me at ten weeks old – or at least that's what it felt like when she arrived.

Sharon Harding of HiBird Photography contributed many of the

▲ *Bringing fun into our lives*

illustrations to this book, especially the step-by-step photos of place-board training. Joe Welling took photos of me with my dogs that didn't actually break the lens. And then there are all the wonderful dog people who have let me use photos of their own dogs and pups. These include: Jennifer and Howard Day; Claire Dunn; Peter Geldard; Laura Woodall; Tarquin Millington-Drake; Frances Draper; Hannah Green; Lucy Dixon; Sherina Balaratnam; James Troughton.

At Quiller Publishing, Andrew Johnston, the managing director, has been tremendously helpful in shaping the book and discussing what dog owners really want from a book, and Camilla Mason has somehow licked the manuscript into shape.

And finally, we must all acknowledge our dogs, who bring such fun (and chaos) into our lives and somehow enable us to be better people as a result of their dogness.

INTRODUCTION

This book tells you the truth about your first puppy that other training manuals leave out. To begin with, I'm going to give you the answers to the very first, basic questions you want to know.

Then, as we solve the immediate pressing problems of toilet training, general confusion and naughtiness, we can move on to all the great fun to be had with a dog growing up in the family.

▶ *Effective training forms a puppy's future*

A while ago my Dad, a hospital doctor (now retired), was lucky enough to be allowed to buy a really fantastic bit of medical kit for the operating suite. The money had been raised and everybody was very excited. Eventually the high-tech equipment arrived all the way from Japan and my Dad was put in charge of opening the box. Pretty quickly he had all the bits out and more or less assembled and was starting to press buttons when he noticed a sheet of paper printed in various different languages. English was the top of the list, and he read: 'In case of extreme emergency, consult instructions.' My Dad confessed: 'Those

Japanese must know surgeons very well; it would certainly take an extreme emergency for me to bother to read the instructions.'

It's not just surgeons. When you get your new mobile phone or tablet, what do you do? Start clicking. Manufacturers of tech devices know this, and design them to pander to our impatience. It's called 'intuitive operation' which basically means you can get started straight away and don't need to bother to read the instructions – unless there's an extreme emergency of course!

It is different with dogs. Nature did not design puppies to have intuitive operation. Just about the only things puppies do automatically are poo and chew. As a townie and a career girl, I didn't have an opportunity to get my first puppy until I was in my thirties. I must admit that in many respects I am my father's daughter, so it didn't occur to me for a moment to read the instructions *before* the arrival of the pup – or even until an extreme emergency arose. So I was left searching around for a decent puppy care handbook, with the said pup already eating her way through the kitchen wall.

I like to think that I'm not the only person in the world to rush ahead and buy a gorgeous little bundle of pup without bothering about the instruction booklet. So I'm guessing there will be plenty of you reading this now with the book or tablet in one hand while trying to rescue the pup from inside the sofa with the other hand. So **Part One** is designed to get you started right away. It is a survival guide which will get you through the first few weeks of puppy management. All your pressing puppy problems will be answered step by step, with simple, direct answers.

You will discover easy to follow routines for toilet training, feeding, playing, and also for teaching your children how to handle a pup. Having already made all the mistakes in the book when I first started with dogs, this book has the answers to those mistakes! I can also reassure you that success is rapid. I'm now on my fifth generation of breeding my line of cocker spaniels, and I'm glad to say that every litter has been better and more enjoyable than the last.

In the book you will see lots of photos of one of my latest pups, Fizz, who was growing up while I was planning *From Puppy to Perfect*. She spent most of her first summer 'glamping' on the lawn in full Glastonbury style. Training her along the lines I will be describing was a total joy, and as I write this, she's now getting ready to go into competitions.

Once you and pup have survived the first few weeks, you will have a moment to step back and think about your longer term plan for owning and training your first puppy to become a perfect companion. So **Part Two** gives an insight into the big picture of dog ownership. We will be looking especially at the human part of the dog–family partnership – because, as you will discover, your puppy ends up teaching you just as much as you train him! If you are one of those sensible people who has bought the book *before* the pup, there is plenty of useful advice on the different types and personalities of dog. This is great when it comes to choosing your dog, and also comes in very handy if the pup is already in place to let you know what to expect from the different breeds as they grow up.

With the puppy now settled, and you briefed with a plan for the future, it's time to move on to **Part Three**, which is a detailed guide on how to look after and introduce play-training for the puppy from now, up to about six months old. Then **Part Four** concentrates on sensible, effective, serious training for your puppy from the age of about six months, forming the foundation for his whole future. This includes a unique masterclass with Britain's most successful gundog trainer, Ian Openshaw, on a brand new method, placeboard training, which he has just introduced from America.

By the time your dog is about a year old, you will both be flying! You will have learnt so much, and not just about dogs and dog training. I found that I discovered just as much about people and families along the way as I did about dogs. This is the moment where you and the dog are in a great position to go ahead and enjoy life together. To get the best out of this future, it's a good idea to think about some hobbies and pursuits you can all do together, so **Part Five** gives a guide to all the many different activities and forms of advanced training the family can enjoy with the dog.

And I have also included a special **Dog Log** section which helps you to build your own profile of your dog to be used if you want to create a web page or blog for him – great fun for the children. It can also be used to generate posters and online alerts, in the very remote possibility that the dog goes missing.

So there is a load to look forward to, but since your pup may already be harassing the hamster at this very moment, let's get started!

PART ONE

THE SIX WEEK SURVIVAL GUIDE

This is your step-by-step guide to surviving your first few weeks as the owner of a not yet perfect puppy. It takes you through from the time that you buy the puppy, which is usually a few weeks before he is ready to leave the breeder, up to the end of your first month of having the puppy at home. By this time your puppy will be three months old and beginning to grow up quite quickly, ready to enter the next stage of his life.

▶ *Don't worry about choosing the right puppy from a litter (or barrel!) – they are all adorable*

DOs and DON'Ts of Buying a Puppy

DO visit the Kennel Club website – details of British and American Kennel Clubs are at the back of this book

DO visit websites of the breed clubs of your favourite types of dog – suggested websites are at the back of this book

DO ask around and get word-of-mouth recommendations

DO visit the breeder before you buy

DO be prepared to pay a reasonable commercial price – breed clubs will give you an idea of how much

DON'T buy puppies straight off the internet

DON'T agree to take a puppy home at younger than eight weeks

DON'T meet the breeder at a 'neutral' place such as motorway service stations, lay-bys, supermarket car parks

DON'T buy a puppy without any paperwork – expect at least a receipt and if the puppy is pure-bred there should be registration details from the Kennel Club

DON'T take children on the first visit as they will fall in love with the puppy and put pressure on you

Puppy Arrival Week (PAW) minus two weeks

Chat with the breeder

Pup will still be with the breeder at this stage and now is the time to have a quick chat with the breeder to make sure you both agree what needs to be done. The breeder will have weaned the pup from his mum and got him onto regular solid foods. It is also the breeder's responsibility to give the puppy a proper worming. It is a fact of life that puppies often have worms! Even the very best, most hygienic kennels can't always eradicate worms completely. The cycle where microscopic worm eggs are carried in the mum's milk and given to the suckling pup is very hard to break. So it is really important for the breeder to worm the puppy when he is being weaned. Check your breeder has done this and keep a note of the wormer used. That means that when you next worm the puppy in a couple of weeks you can alternate brands as advised by your vet. Reputable breeders will be quite happy to supply this information.

Breeders are not usually responsible for the vaccinations of your new pup. These generally take place after the pup has arrived home with you. However some breeders agree to keep the puppy with them for two or three extra weeks and do the vaccination programme during this time. This can be very helpful if for any reason you can't pick up the puppy at the normal eight-week-old stage. Obviously if you make this arrangement with the breeder then you must expect to pay more to cover the cost of vaccination and keep fees. The best dog breeders are not out to make huge profits from breeding and rarely charge enough extra to cover more than the bare cost of vet's fees, let alone including their own labour costs.

▶ *This is what you will fall in love with!*

I recently accepted a puppy from a litter fathered by my stud dog, FTCh Gournaycourt Ginger, instead of a stud fee. When the lovely breeders, Roy and Sandra Ellershaw, delivered my pup to me, everything except vaccination had been taken care of. The little pup was even more or less house-trained, as well as being drop-dead gorgeous! This is the kind of service to expect from a Kennel Club 'assured breeder' or similar. If you use the Kennel Club or breed clubs to find your breeder, it will make life much easier. Buying a puppy advertised online can be risky and won't give you the kind of guarantees you get from properly established breeding organisations.

▼ *Pup can learn the 'sit' at just a few weeks old*

Now is the time to organise with the breeder the date you will collect the pup. Make sure it's a day when you are not too busy. Dealing with a carsick puppy doesn't work well with presenting an important business proposal!

Get Kitted Up

You will need:

1. Stacks and stacks of old newspapers (start collecting now!)

2. A medium-size plastic washable dog bed – if you are buying a breed that will grow up to be very large, you may have to increase the size of the dog bed as your puppy grows

3. Washable dog bedding fleece (Vetbed or similar)

4. Two stainless steel water bowls

5. Two stainless steel feed bowls

6. A puppy collar with tag and clip-on lead

7. An indoor dog pen – this is a large, foldable, wire pen which will become your pup's bedroom throughout its life (see back of book for supplier websites)

8. A puppy playpen – not vital but really nice to have a collapsible playpen which can keep your puppy safe anywhere in the house or garden when you can't keep an eye on him (see back of book for supplier websites)

9. Some puppy-safe chew sticks (your vet will supply)

10. Food as recommended by the breeder

11. Basic grooming kit of brush, comb, tooth brush, ear cleanser

12. And of course, a cuddly toy or two!

Puppy-proof house and garden

Bringing a puppy home is a bit like a basic version of bringing a baby home. Don't make the mistake of thinking 'he's only a puppy, what can he do?' because the tiniest puppy is capable of wreaking devastation on a scale completely disproportionate to his size. When Solo was a little pup he had his bed and play area in the cloakroom, with a playpen to prevent him getting into the lavatory. This went fine for the first couple of weeks. But Solo was busy growing. The day he discovered he could climb out over the playpen happened to be the day I was in London visiting an editor. I got home to discover Solo sitting in the lavatory bowl surrounded by loo paper, in a scene like an Andrex advert directed by Quentin Tarantino. Thank heavens he hadn't discovered the bleach bottle.

If there is trouble to be got into, your puppy will get into it. When you are puppy-proofing just think of a baby at the crawling/toddling/investigating stage and you will know what to do. Generally put things out of reach; make sure doors and cupboards close properly; don't leave anything you care about within access.

One of the most frequent questions I get asked is: 'how do I stop my puppy from chewing everything in sight?' to which the answer is very simple: 'don't leave anything in sight.' If you don't want your puppy to chew an item, don't leave it where he can chew it! Puppies do need to chew though, especially when they are teething, so make sure there are plenty of nice, safe things available for your puppy to chew. I like to let my pups chew on small rag chews available from vets, pet shops and supermarkets. I also give them old socks, which they much prefer to any bought toys and which are very useful for play-training. Puppy will delight in gardening gloves, so you may as well just let him have them.

Edible chews are useful, but don't let your puppy have them very often when he is young, as they can upset his stomach. I also tend to avoid very squeaky toys. My puppies will grow up to compete in disciplines where hard mouthing and biting of objects is discouraged, and I have found that a pup gets in the habit of biting the toy in order to get it to squeak. The squeak-makers themselves can be dangerous if swallowed, and of course, the perpetual shrieking of puppy's plastic brontosaurus can wear thin very quickly.

Do pay special attention to puppy-proofing the garden. There are a number of reasons for this. Number one of course, you don't want him getting out and into next door or worse still, onto the road. So make sure there are no holes, no matter how tiny, that he can squeeze through. If the garden is open plan, then you will need a playpen or to build a little dog run. While the puppy is still small, the run doesn't have to be very much larger than you would have for other family pets, like a rabbit or guinea pig. You can see Fizz's 'glamping' run in the photo. Do remember that you must have shade or shelter, water and a bed for the pup – although you don't need to go to the lengths of including their own private swimming pool, as Fizz had for her first summer!

Please don't even consider any electric collar boundary or fencing you may see advertised. There's a discussion of this kind of device later in the book. For now, just trust me, and don't even think about it.

▼ *Fizz 'glamping' on the lawn, Glastonbury-style*

PAW minus one week

Create puppy palace

It is really important for a puppy, and a grown-up dog, to have his own space within the house, or possibly outside if he is a breed more suited to living in a purpose-built kennel. Dogs are just like humans in this. They need their own place to go and chill. Your teenager sulks in his bedroom. You fling yourself down in the living room. Your mother-in-law moulders at the kitchen table. Husbands notoriously hide in the shed. Your puppy may very well join you in all these places, but he also needs somewhere that is his very own space where he can feel secure and relaxed.

We will discover later in the book how important this canine bedroom is when it comes to training your dog. Right from the very beginning though, it helps in giving your pup a sense of feeling grounded. Pups who have their own pads grow up to be confident and relaxed as adult dogs.

▶ *Sealyham pups enjoy a more luxurious outdoor puppy palace*

▶ *The pup box can go indoors or out depending on the weather*

The first time I bred a litter of pups I based the mum up in the spare room where it would be quiet for her. After days of traipsing up and down with cups of coffee to drink while I sat with her, I realised my mistake. Now all my litters are born in close proximity to the kettle!

A fully set-up puppy palace is illustrated here. The floor is lined with newspaper for the occasional accident. Half the pen is occupied by the bed, lined with washable bedding. The other half has pup's water bowl, and of course, lots of toys. The door of the pen is open to allow pup access to a larger play area. I also have a barrier around this area at first, to help with training and prevent the pup getting into mischief. At night, or when the pup will be alone for a little while, the door of the pen is closed to encourage him to settle down in his bed for a rest.

▲ *This safe, warm place was used for a whelping and now doubles as pup's first home*

Chat with the children

Excitement is going to be running high as Puppy Arrival Day draws near. Of course you want your children to enjoy the new four-legged family member; that's probably why you decided to get a pup in the first place. But if you have very young or boisterous children, there do need to be a few boundaries, particularly while the children get used to having a dog.

Sit the kids down for a chat. If the kids won't sit down long enough for a chat, I'm afraid that doesn't look hopeful for the future. Children need to know about boundaries and respect. Having an animal in the house is a really good way of teaching these qualities. Your children need to understand that the puppy is a real, living creature, not a computer game or a toy. There will be times when the puppy is too tired for them to play with him, and they must respect that. He will need to be handled quite gently to begin with – he's only very young. And if you need to remind the children about this occasionally, they must take it on board – a family lucky enough to have a lovely puppy is not a sulky family!

A family came to see one of my litters a little while ago, and the two children were stroppy almost from the outset. They insisted on holding a puppy each. Naturally enough one of the puppies had a little widdle while the daughter was holding him. She let out a screech like a female tennis player and instantly threw the tiny pup away. Thank heavens I managed to catch him as he plummeted towards the stone-flagged kitchen floor. When I refused to let the family have a pup Mum and Dad were stunned, and all four of them were still sulking as they made their way back to the car!

Do the admin

Consider whether you are going to insure the puppy against vet's fees. If you buy your pup from a Kennel Club breeder you will get free introductory insurance covering your first two weeks of ownership. There are pros and cons to continuing the insurance. Insurance companies are not charities, so remember they will make a profit overall out of the service they provide. If you have bought a hardy breed of dog that almost never needs the vet, you are likely to be the person providing the profit! But if you have a breed that is more prone to health problems or is very valuable, then it could be worthwhile. Ask around and look online to see what the health profile of your breed is. My spaniels are toughies and just visit the vet once a year for their annual check-up and booster – needless to say this is not covered by insurance. The last unscheduled visit to the vet was when Bisto was truffling around on the beach and managed to get an enormous rusty fish hook through his lip. My wonderful vet extracted it with pliers, and Bisto was such a brave soldier the vet let me off the consultation charge! Most terriers are also pretty hardy – although you might consider additional insurance for all the stuff they steal or destroy!

Register with a good local vet – ask your friends with animals who they recommend. Don't be too impressed with state-of-the-art facilities which are expensive, and you hope you will never need to use. Instead make sure your vet actually likes dogs. Believe it or not, this isn't always the case! Clean, friendly and nearby are my priorities when choosing a vet. Book your puppy in for his first visit. This is usually at ten weeks old when your vet will give the puppy a general health check and start the vaccination programme – although some vets have a slightly different routine. You should also get a very useful introduction pack and possibly some free samples! It's a good idea to register with the vet in person rather than over the phone or online because then you can pick up the recommended wormer and flea products that you will need.

Prepare the car

Although puppy is very likely to spend his first car journey sitting on the non-driver's knee in a nest of towels, this isn't the recommended procedure permanently. For most of us with hatchbacks, people carriers and 4x4s, the back is the place for the dog. By far the best way for your puppy and grown dog to travel is in a dog pen specially designed for the car. You will see the nation's dogs travelling in state in these as you crawl up the motorway. I always envy my dogs in their pen. It takes up the whole of the back of the 4x4 so they can stand up and turn round and have a shake and a scratch. Plus they have their own bedding, non-spill water bowl and side vent windows open. Far more comfortable in a traffic jam than the rest of us squashed up at the front with no wriggle room and all hot and sticky!

Other options for in-car travel include dog guards which separate the back from the passenger seats, and there are even canine seat belts. If it will fit, you can also use your pup's indoor dog pen in the back of the vehicle. But the purpose-built dog traveller is the best option if you have space and money for it (the

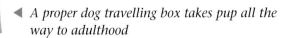

◀ *A proper dog travelling box takes pup all the way to adulthood*

back of the book lists websites were you can find good deals and second-hand travelling pens). If you are ever unlucky enough to have an accident, the travelling pen is much safer for both the dog and you.

When I first started with dogs, it was the custom for the dog to travel in the footwell of the front passenger seat. Depending on your dog, this has many drawbacks. It is unsafe, as in the event of an accident your unfortunate dog becomes a missile, with risk of injury to himself and you. Most dogs will intermittently climb out of the footwell onto the passenger seat, which they will trash with their muddy paws, and chew the strap of your designer handbag as you desperately attempt to push the dog back down off the seat while driving round a roundabout. Unsurprisingly the police take a dim view of this, and you can be fined for not having the dog under safe control. My first pup, Tara, used to start every journey in

▼ *This vehicle has been well set up for older dogs, with an internal liner and tray, but for pups and long journeys, a good quality dog guard or a dog box is preferable*

the passenger footwell, but would usually end up in the driver footwell, making gear changes a rather random operation. The day she happened to be lying across the dashboard in front of the steering wheel, as a police car drove past, was the day I bought a proper travelling pen.

Do take your breed type into account when making travel arrangements for your dog. If you are buying a toy breed like a pug or a Chihuahua, these are not called handbag dogs for nothing! They will be very happy in a little travelling house held in place on the back seat using the safety belt. There are lots of these dog carriers available online, and I have been told that pugs really do express a preference about which decoration they like best! The larger breeds, like Labradors, can often be poor travellers, with a tendency to carsickness and hyper-salivation (slobber) on car journeys. So although they are not restless, they need proper travel arrangements.

It is important that active, inquisitive breeds like collies and spaniels are safely confined. A young couple came to pick up brother and sister pups from me which I had kept on to ten weeks old for them. As we arranged pick-up day, my last words over the phone were: 'Remember to have a proper travelling pen – those dog guards are useless for this breed.' The couple arrived, sure enough, with a cheap and cheerful dog guard separating the hatchback from the rest of the car. The two young pups were placed in the hatchback and the couple shook hands with me and got into the car, whereupon they found each of the front seats filled by a puppy. That was how long it took for the pups to dismantle the dog guard and climb through.

Puppy Arrival Day

Collecting puppy

Having a new puppy is about the best fun I can think of. There's all the cooing and cuddling and excitement of a baby without the general exhaustion and stress. So don't let yourself spoil that great experience by being disorganised and chaotic. Start as you mean to go on by setting out in good time to arrive at the breeder when expected. I very rarely sell any pups, but when I do I make sure everything is absolutely ready for the pup's new owner. Here's what I do: I prepare a puppy pack containing a week's supply of the puppy's food; all the Kennel Club documentation including pedigree and insurance scheme; a 'what to do' list for the first few days; puppy's favourite toy and his bedding. Just before the buyer is going to arrive I take the puppy out for a lavatory run. I adjust his feeding so that his tummy won't be so full as to get upset on the journey, or so empty that he gets very hungry. I will give him a short playtime so that he is a little bit sleepy for the journey. Here's what the new owners do: they arrive about two hours late, in a great rush and hurry. By this time the best moment for the pup to travel has long gone. So do yourself a favour, and arrive in time and calm!

Welcome home!

Hopefully your journey will have gone smoothly, with pup snoozing either on the passenger's lap or in his car travelling pen. When you arrive at your house carry the pup into the garden first to give him a few moments to have a wee. This is a routine you are going to get used to! Don't worry if he doesn't go, and don't hang around waiting until he gets tired and chilly. Most pups will have a little widdle instantly. Then it's back into the house and, boringly, straight into his puppy palace for a rest. Put the toy and bedding from the breeder in with him and make sure his water bowl is full. The puppy needs a bit of time just now to rest physically from the journey, and mentally to adjust to his new surroundings. Frustratingly, this isn't the moment for you and the family to be passing him from hand to hand and having cuddles. The best thing to do is just watch him for a bit. Sit yourself down in the comfy chair – now you discover why you were recommended to put it there – and just watch puppy for a while. The family can take it in turns if they must. Expect your pup to toddle around his pen a bit and then curl up (usually somewhere completely bizarre like in the feed bowl – it's very unlikely to be in the bed) for a little sleep. There may be a bit of whimpering. Don't worry, it's not something you need to do anything about.

Once pup has fallen asleep, you all need to leave him in peace for a while. Maybe tiptoe up and have a silent 'aaah' but that's all. I find the hardest aspect of any in dog training, is knowing that your pup or dog needs his own time and space, and having the self-discipline to back off and give it to him. If you have young children, they will find this difficult too. It is really important though, and we will be finding out why in Part Two.

How to pick up and hold puppy

When the puppy wakes up and is ready to come and play, he will let you know! Even if you aren't right by the pen, the general crashing about and charming whirring sounds of a puppy trying to bark will alert you. So pick him up and take him briefly outside for a lavatory break. When picking up puppies you need to be careful to protect their joints and internal organs. While the pup is still very tiny, most breeds will be small enough to sit supported in the palm of your hand as illustrated.

For larger breeds, and as pup grows up, you can hold him on your arm and hand. His rib-cage and tummy is supported by your forearm, with his legs either side, and his head and neck rest in your up-turned hand, as illustrated. For more security, and cuddles, hold the puppy close to your body. Holding your pup like this not only protects his internal organs, but it gives you very good control over him if he has a tendency to be a bit wriggly or chewy.

When picking up your puppy, start by sliding your hand round underneath his body so you can ease him into the correct holding position. Involve your children in learning how to do this and explain to them why it is important for puppy to be held safely. As the puppy gets older he will get much stronger and will usually be pretty bouncy, so the time for boisterous games will arrive very quickly.

At any age it is important to be careful when picking

◀ *Firm but gentle holding makes sure this tiny puppy can't accidentally wriggle free*

▲ *A good way of carrying a pup with support and control*

▲ *A less conventional method, but still makes sure pup's internal organs are not pressured*

up and carrying dogs as it is surprisingly easy to cause an injury by random grabbing. Aim to pick up a dog by sliding both hands under his front legs and holding his chest, as shown. You have good control of the dog, and if by any chance he is being naughty, it's also a good way of reminding him who is boss. Another good way of picking up and carrying a dog, especially if he is bigger, older or may be unwell, is to embrace all four legs at once and lift up the body. For tough working breeds that might need to be grabbed out of deep undergrowth or when they are very muddy, you can use the two skin folds – one at the scruff of the neck and the other on the rump – and lift the dog with a firm, but not pinching, grip on those folds. When a friend first saw me lugging one of my truly filthy dogs into the back of the 4x4 by this method, she said: 'It's not a suitcase!' but in fact healthy dogs don't find this uncomfortable at all. Puppies of course have been used to mum carrying them by the scruff of the neck from the beginning.

First feed

The pup's breeder will have given you some guidelines on how and when to feed the pup, along with a supply of food to carry you over the transition phase. Don't be tempted to overfeed your puppy on day one, and certainly don't give him any treats or snacks. It's a massive change in environment for the puppy to get used to and his digestion and appetite will reflect this. He may go off his food and have an upset tum. This is perfectly normal and usually settles down within twenty-four hours. If he is off food and has an upset tum, a little chopped chicken breast or rice pudding or some scrambled egg will usually put things right. For his first couple of feeds, put the bowl in his puppy palace with him and give him time to eat it at his own pace. Take any leftover food away the following morning. Once the pup has settled in he will be scarfing down his food at a great pace – this is when you can start using the feed bowl for training purposes, which we will discuss later on.

The first two weeks at home

Feeding routine

It's a good idea to feed the pup four small meals a day at first, and reduce that to two meals a day when it reaches the age of about three months or so. My adult dogs are fed twice a day. Even more important than how often you feed the pup is to stick to a routine. Please feed the pup at the same times every day. A good feed schedule is breakfast; lunch; children's tea-time (about 4 or 5pm); and finally mid-evening (about 8pm). Whatever schedule you decide on, stick to it! Why? Because a pup who is fed regularly will digest regularly, and therefore move his bowels regularly. And regular, predictable bowel movements will make your life so much easier! I know this does rather apply universally and the thing about having a young puppy in the house is that you just can't get away from the fact that what goes in one end, will in due course come out the other!

If you forget to feed pup at lunchtime and then suddenly remember in the evening that you have forgotten and so give it a big meal then, you are going to wake up to a dirty protest the following morning. By feeding regularly you can establish the pup on a toilet cycle that you can actually predict most of the time.

Toilet training

As you can tell from the above, successful toilet training is all about establishing the right routines. The better and more consistent your routine, the easier it will be to house-train your dog. First of all ask yourself what is the first thing you do when you wake up in the morning? Your puppy is no different. While he is still very young he can't be expected to cross his legs and wait for you to take him out, so you will have to make his toilet trip a priority – yes, before you put the kettle on.

So first thing, pup goes out for a quick wee. Then, throughout the day, here are the moments to take him outside. Every time you or the family are going to pick him up and play with him, out he goes first. It doesn't take long; he'll quickly have a little wee. Then, any time you are going to put him down to rest in his pen for a while, pop outside with him for a moment before you leave him. And always last thing at night before you all go to bed.

A young pup won't go through the night without a wee, so depending on where you want your pup to relieve himself in the future, there are a couple of things to do. If you plan on leaving him shut in his puppy palace overnight, which I tend to do, then you need to get up during the night and pop downstairs to let him out. It doesn't take very long before pups are able to go through the night, so it isn't a huge commitment, and well worth it in the long term. If you really don't want to get up, or your pup will grow up in an urban environment where he has to use an indoor loo, then you should create an accessible loo area outside his pen – this is described in the special section below for urban dogs.

There will be accidents at first – that's what the newspaper is for! Very young pups still have small bladders and seem to be on 'continuous pour' to begin with, but as long as you are disciplined with the routine, toilet training will only take a matter of days. The most important thing is not to let the pup get in the habit of wetting in his pen or bed. So if there is an accident, be sure to clean out all bedding very thoroughly and use a specialist spray to take the smell away. If the pup can smell his wee it will encourage him to wee again in the same place. Nature is on your side though – no animal wants to soil its own bed. If your pup is difficult to train, then I'm afraid you need to look closely at your routines and make sure you are sticking to them. Just a week of being really scrupulous now is going to make life so much easier in the future.

Hopefully your pup will do his poos at the same time as his widdle run. If you are sticking to the very regular feed times, it should all work quite naturally. I have found, though, that if there is going to be a problem, these first few days are when it happens. First of all puppy digestive systems can be a bit random. And when pup is excited he tends to forget that it's time to move his bowels and only remember again when he's back in his pen to rest – the opposite of what we want! So take pup outside but don't play immediately; try not to stimulate him at all. Don't make eye contact, you'll just have to watch him out of the corner of your eye. After a bit of a run round, he should calm down enough to poo. While he is moving his bowels, encourage him by using a catch phrase. Most people say something like, 'Get busy' or 'Time for business'. The idea is that the pup will learn by association and eventually just the words will trigger him to want to go. There isn't much real science on this though, and I haven't found that it works for all pups.

More important is to remember not to rush indoors the moment he has done his business. After half an hour spent pacing the garden in the pouring rain and howling gale waiting for your puppy to oblige, it is only natural to want to pick him up the instant he has done the deed and rush indoors for a cuppa. Resist this! From the puppy's point of view, he is being punished for pooing. Here's how it goes. Puppy doesn't mind the weather at all. Nor does he get bored hanging around in the garden; he loves it. What he experiences is that the moment he has moved his bowels, being outside playing and truffling around stops and he ends up back indoors. So, in order to prolong his playtime, he will hold on as long as he possibly can before pooing. And five minutes turns into ten and drags into twenty and you get colder and more desperate! You may even give up and go back indoors with him, at which point he will promptly poo on the kitchen floor. Preventing this is simple. Once pup has pooed, praise him verbally, and then spend a few moments playing with him – chucking his favourite toy or letting him chase you or similar. Establish this routine and you will soon find that pup does his business as soon as he possibly can so that he can get on with the playing.

Wherever pup is – in the kitchen, the garden or later when he is out on a walk – he will very often give you signals that he wants to poo. Being alert to signals is really helpful in preventing accidents. The first sign is that pup stops what he is doing. Many young pups tend to get a rather charmingly puzzled expression on their face! It seems to say: 'Hmm, strange feeling, I think I want to do something but what can it be?' Most of the time you will have just seconds to act between seeing this expression, and pup realising what he wants to do and proceeding to do it! This is the moment to pick him up and take him outside. Other signs, as the pup gets a little older, are that he will suddenly bark for no apparent reason, or may even go to the door and scratch it. The door scratchers tend to be very intelligent and cooperative dogs who are observing your human behaviour as much as you are observing them. Please don't ignore their signals; it's quite rude if you think about it! The final, last minute warning, that things are about to go 'poo-maggedon', is when the pup starts twirling on the spot, and many dogs continue to have a preparatory twirl throughout their lives.

I'm sorry to dwell on poo (not literally!), but there is no getting away from it – and that *is* literally the case when you are out and about with your dog and have to scoop his poo into a little plastic bag. I met a very nice lady out walking her dog the other day, carrying the obligatory warm bag of poo. She was amazed to hear that if you toilet train your dog properly you will only need to poop scoop when you are on long journeys away from home. Before heading out for walks and adventures, toilet-trained dogs do their poo in a corner of the garden where you can dispose of it with a shovel later.

Mounds and mounds are written about house-training dogs, and people get very stressed about it. But difficulty with house-training is actually not really the problem, but the symptom of more basic issues about how you and the family interact with the new dog in your life. We'll be discussing this in more detail in Part Two.

Urban dogs and dog owners in Europe don't get it at all when British and American people stress over toilet training. A wander along any Parisian boulevard or Italian piazza makes it perfectly clear that a little sh** is considered just part of the street furniture. But really, the place for poo is in the loo! Rural dogs (like mine) leave their droppings in agricultural fields where they mix in with all the other forms of dung making such a rich tapestry of our countryside. Suburban dogs usually use the back garden (or sometimes a specially designated area in a local park) where poo can be safely cleared away. Truly urban dogs don't have these options, so they have to be trained to use a dog lavatory in the house, and I suppose if cats and humans can manage to learn to do it, pups can as well!

There are lots of versions of indoor dog loos including trays and pads. Check out the various options and websites listed at the back of the book. Decide where you want your pup's loo to be. It is a good idea to create a puppy area within the home. This will be his puppy palace where his bed and toys are, along with an extended play area or pen which he can access at any time, but which he can't escape from into the rest of the flat or house. Put his loo in this extended area. Once he has used this loo a couple of times, he will learn to use it always. In some respects, urban dog owners don't have to work so hard on toilet training, because the pup always has access to his loo and you don't physically have to take him outside all the time. The downside of course, is that you will have to clean up his poo for always, whereas the rural dog owner just considers his dog's dump to be a contribution to the cycle of life!

Show consideration about poo bags

While most of us have taken on board the fact that when out walking, we need to pick up and put our dog's poo in a bag, some people don't seem to realise that our social responsibility doesn't end there. Putting poo in a plastic bag is not enough. You must then dispose of the plastic bag in the bin provided by the local council. If there is no bin, unfortunately you will have to take the poo bag home and dispose of it there. Hanging a bag of poo from a nearby tree or leaving it at the side of the footpath just makes it worse. Now we have a non-biodegradable plastic bag litter problem in addition to the poo. Poo left alone washes away in the next rain. Poo in a plastic bag decorating a tree can last for several months. Yuck!

Puppy's name

Most puppies seem to select their own names. Ginger got his name from his magnificent ginger eyebrows, which you can see in the photo. That meant that his sisters also had to be spices, so we had Pepper, Nutmeg and Posh! As a puppy, Fizz was a champagne blonde, and arrived home in Royal Ascot week just as the fizz was being uncorked.

Surprisingly though, you can make some real howlers when it comes to naming your pup. Bisto's litter also included Marmite, Bovril, Spud and Gravy – who had to be renamed! The name you give your pup says a lot about how you feel about him. A pretentious name (and Cadbury is not as imaginative a name for a chocolate Labrador as you might think) seems to be inflicted on the pup without taking his personality into account. It says the owner is more important than the dog. Joke names (like Gravy!) can also rebound. The equestrian three-day-event rider Lucinda Green had a terrier-cross which she called Basil after *Fawlty Towers*. Basil turned out rather a naughty dog, and the joke of constantly shrieking 'Baaasil!' after him wore rather thin. When I named Ricky after my friend's well-known winning springer, I did worry about the *EastEnders* connection. Fortunately my Ricky has turned out so impeccably behaved that you only ever hear the R of the Ricky. So do put a little thought into your dog's name, as it will set the tone of this future training.

Start using your pup's name straight away. He will learn it very quickly. Your pup's name is actually the very first piece of training you do with him. Saying his name is a form of communication, and how you say it can be anything from an instruction or command; to a telling off; to a soothing reassurance. For something so important, it is wonderful that it is so easy, and pups seem to take to it instantly.

When you are playing with your pup on the floor, just say his name and perhaps wave his favourite toy, and you will find he immediately comes waddling up to you. This is actually the foundation of the 'come' instruction that you will teach more formally later on. You will find that your puppy is instinctively really engaged with you at this young age, and therefore wants to come and see you and do what you ask him to if he can work out what that is. With a little care, you can build naturally on this so that your pup grows up to be a perfect, obedient, happy dog without either of you ever really feeling you have had to put any effort into training.

So, at this early stage, use his name when you are playing, and encourage him to come to you when he hears his name. Be very careful not to confuse him by having lots of people yelling his name all the time. And when you do use his name, pay attention to him. Don't call him over and then ignore him – he'll soon stop coming! Don't repeatedly say his name, say his name, say his name, say his name, so often that he switches off to it, just as you probably did halfway through that sentence. If he ignores his name, and has definitely heard it and knows it is his name, just go quietly over to him and pick him up for a cuddle and repeat his name. A pup who always pays attention when it hears his name, is already halfway to being trained. You won't believe it, but if you just concentrate a bit at this stage, it is that easy.

Visiting the vet

Pup's first vet appointment will usually come round at the end of his second week at home, with the follow-up ten days to a fortnight later. As well as being important for vaccinations, the visit is a chance for you to learn from the vet. You can discuss feeding, and anything you might be worrying about. The vet will also check the puppy's general health including ears and teeth. The vet will probably suggest having your pup microchipped if this has not already been done by the breeder. It is extremely cheap and means that your dog will be easily identifiable for the rest of his life. This is tremendously helpful if the dog ever strays or even gets stolen. The UK government has recently announced that it is preparing legislation requiring all dogs to be microchipped. Some breeds already have to be microchipped by law. These are working dogs like spaniels, who are required to go into thick undergrowth and often damage their tails. The tip of the tail is removed by a vet when the pup is three days old and it is then microchipped and entered into the legal registry of 'docked breeds'.

It will be puppy's first outing, the beginning of his socialisation programme. Make sure he's done a recent widdle and poo before you set out and don't feed him too close to the journey or appointment time. Remember he doesn't have full immunity from illness at this stage, so even though everyone in the waiting room will want to cuddle him, and other dogs sniff him, it isn't a good idea – people will understand.

Toys and play

As your puppy grows up, he's going to learn through playing. This is great because it means you are both going to have great fun, but it also means his toys are not just his toys. Many of the toys he plays with, like tennis balls, rolled up socks and raggers, will become training aids in the weeks to come. It means you and the family have to be a bit more careful about toys than you would think. It's a bit like when your child gets her first junior tablet device – it's a wonderful toy she will enjoy, and it is a fantastic learning aid, but it is also a serious bit of kit that does need some supervising.

Surprisingly, although it's not as high-tech as a tablet, the good old-fashioned tennis ball plays a similar role for your puppy. He loves playing with it as a toy, but it is also going to be an aid to teaching him how to be obedient; how to have self-control and discipline; and maybe one day to join in competition or working spheres like obedience trialling or even to become a search and rescue dog. So that trusty old tennis ball needs to be treated with care!

Have plenty of cuddly toys that your pup keeps with him in his pen, and in his first couple of weeks these will be the toys you all play with. Avoid doing tug-of-war as this can harm the pup's teeth and the shape of his jaw. It also encourages him to hold on to items rather than giving them to you, which you are more likely to want him to do. Keep the tennis balls and throwing toys separate in a little bag. Roll a tennis ball for your pup and play with him as he chases it and tries to get it back to you. You can also hide it all over the place and play searching games.

Don't overdo any of these games, and don't let the rest of the family overdo it either. You should never reach the stage when your puppy is too bored or tired to want to play. A puppy that doesn't play can't learn. It's hard, but try to restrain yourself from jazzing him up too much either. My cocker spaniels seem to come pre-jazzed, and our early play lessons usually consist of them whirling round the kitchen, seemingly at head height, while I hopelessly try to calm things down. This isn't recommended. Just like the bored puppy, the overexcited puppy isn't in the right frame of mind to learn either.

Puppy downtime

Just like a small child, pups need loads of rest too. This is where his puppy palace really comes into its own. You want your puppy's downtime to coincide with times when you are too busy with something else to pay him full attention. The puppy palace will allow you to plan and control puppy's downtimes. You will find that when you pop him into his pen, he will play with his toys and chunter around a bit, before quite happily settling himself down for a rest. This will give you the opportunity to get on with rewiring the house; cooking dinner; doing Pilates or whatever it is that puppy can't join in with.

Playing with you and the family is very stimulating for a puppy. While whizzing round interacting with you all, he is also learning huge amounts very quickly, and inside his puppy brain, all sorts of new neural pathways are firing up. Just as it is for a child, this is mentally tiring. It is also physically tiring, as the puppy is being handled and doing a lot of movement. So it is important not to overdo it. Some larger breeds, like Labradors, need plenty of rest while they are physically growing. The bones and joints must be allowed to strengthen before they are stressed, otherwise defects can arise. Even small breeds shouldn't be over-exercised when they are young. Your vet or the breed society will advise the right levels of activity and exercise.

Make sure the family respects puppy's downtime. Let him wake up naturally rather than diving in and pulling him out of his bed every five minutes. Pestering a tired puppy is a jolly good way of encouraging him to be snappy.

The next two weeks

Grooming

Young pups are groomed brilliantly by their mothers. When they first arrive home they are clean and lovely and smell delicious! And at first they don't get out into the thick of things very much, and so they do tend to stay quite nice. But now is the time to get them used to being groomed. The type and amount of grooming you have to do in the future will vary tremendously across the different breeds of dog. A lot of my country friends have working dogs that just get hosed down every few weeks whether they need it or not! This will obviously not work if the dog is going to be allowed in the sitting room. If you have a breed with a spectacular coat, like a Hungarian puli (think Dougal from *Magic Roundabout*) or a bichon frisé, you are going to spend a lot of time grooming your dog. Check the website for your breed. Do bear grooming in mind when you are choosing your breed.

For most breeds, and pretty much all pups at the very beginning, all you will need is a soft brush to get them used to the sensation of being brushed. Gently use a small comb or wire brush to tease out any tangles. Check pup's ears very carefully to make sure there are no little mites. If your pup is rapidly developing a lot of ear wax that can be a sign of ear mites. Start play-cleaning your pup's teeth so he will be used to it with his adult teeth. Run your hands against the grain of the pup's fur to check if there are any lice or other creepy-crawlies. Grass seeds can also work their way deep into the fur and cause problems. Check pup's paws very carefully to make sure no grass seeds or other foreign bodies have got lodged in there. Make sure pup's eyes are clear and not runny.

Many pups (and adult dogs) like to roll in stuff. I won't go into details about the kind of stuff they like to roll in. Let's just say that if it happens, you will want to wash your pup! While pups are still small, I use the kitchen sink. Half fill it with lukewarm water and stand the puppy in it, with a fairly firm grip, as chaos may break out. Using a cup or the tap, get him wet all over up to his neck. Now use a small amount of specialist dog shampoo to work into his coat. Don't be tempted to use washing-up liquid or human shampoo. Dogs' coats are very different from human hair and they can often have surprisingly sensitive skin. Rinse very thoroughly and drain the sink. Before you let puppy out of the sink, dry him as much as you can. There are special super-absorbent towels available which are excellent. The reason you want pup as dry as possible is because the moment he goes down onto the kitchen floor he is going to go mental! He will run around shaking and rubbing himself against you and the furniture and the cat, and generally behaving like a clown. This mad moment is hilarious and enjoyable for all – provided you are prepared for it.

The feed bowl lesson

This is the very first proper lesson for the puppy, and it happens every feeding time from now onwards. For the first few days after puppy's arrival home, you probably gave him his food in his puppy palace or his playpen, and maybe left him with it for a bit to give him time to get interested in it and finish eating. Now that puppy is settled in, he will be eating all his food immediately, every time you feed him, and will probably be pestering you for the feed bowl. Fast-growing young pups always get very hungry – and most breeds stay that way! Owners of the gundog and hound breed groups especially will know that their dogs seem to be permanently hungry.

Once your pup is eating regularly and well, it is time to introduce the feed bowl lesson. Don't try to do it immediately; for it to work you need him to be relaxed, and moderately hungry! Decide where he is going to be fed from now onwards – probably in the kitchen, but it can be anywhere that suits your lifestyle. Prepare his food and take it over to his feeding station. I expect puppy will be there before you, with his eyes already on the feed bowl. Normally you would give him his feed immediately, but now you are going to use his interest in the feed bowl to give him his first proper lesson, which is how to sit and wait.

Hold the feed bowl above his head, at roughly your chest height. The vast majority of pups will naturally want to look upwards to keep the feed bowl in sight, and as their little heads go up, so their bums automatically go down to the floor, and they end up in sitting position.

As you hold the bowl up, give the instruction that you are going to give for 'sit'. Most people will use the word 'sit', but some breeds have other words traditionally associated with the instruction. Spaniel owners, for example, say 'hup'. You might want to use a completely different word,perhaps if English is not your mother tongue. All that matters is that the word is short, easy to say, easy to remember and very distinctive. This book assumes you will be using 'sit'. Once puppy has sat, which will usually be immediately, praise him verbally at the same time as giving him his food. So he is both praised by the boss and rewarded with food when he finds himself in this sitting position.

Every time you feed pup, the routine is the same: bowl above head, and 'sit' instruction; pup's head goes up, bum hits floor, and you have a dog which has in effect obeyed the instruction to 'sit'. It really doesn't matter why he's done it, or even that he knows what he's done. The idea is for it to get hardwired into puppy's brain. Hear the word 'sit'; so sit; then get reward. This very simple lesson is going to set the tone for all your later training of the dog. It is easy for both you and the dog to learn, and it is so straightforward and uncomplicated that there is very little room for anything to go wrong. We don't want either you or the dog to have to think about things. As far as possible, everything will be completely natural and automatic. This means that the dog isn't being asked to make choices. 'Sit' goes straight into his factory settings, so that he finds himself sitting without any obvious thought process. This is good, because dogs are not generally great thinkers! We humans aren't always either, so the more that is pre-programmed, the better. The last thing you want is a situation where you are trying to give the dog an instruction and you can't remember exactly how to do it, and the dog is taking the opportunity to pretend not to understand, or even making his own decision about whether or not to do as you ask.

Do the 'feed bowl sit' every time you feed puppy, and gradually start waiting a little longer before praising him and giving him the feed bowl. After a few days, you will find he is sat down in front of you looking imploringly up at you and waiting for the bowl for really quite a while!

The next stage is to keep him sitting up even after you have put the feed bowl down. Again this is quite simple to achieve. Get him sat. Don't praise yet, and move to put the bowl down. He will immediately break for the bowl, so snatch it up again and repeat the sit command.

As soon as he sits back up, give him the bowl and praise him. Gradually the pup will learn to wait a moment even as the bowl is going to the floor. Now you can get to the final stage of the lesson.

Sit puppy up as normal. This time put the feed bowl down slightly behind and to the left of you, without praising. Some, less bold, pups may instinctively wait to hear praise before they go for the bowl. The more normal, run-about type of pup will head for the bowl, but since you are between him and the bowl, you can physically put a hand between him and the bowl, and hold him while repeating the word 'sit'. Once he has sat, praise him and let him head for the bowl. In a really surprisingly short space of time you will have a puppy who sits obediently and remains sitting even once his feed bowl has been put down, before you release him with praise. I also have a release phrase which I introduce at this stage. It is usually along the lines of 'take it' or 'eat up'.

It's a bit of a party trick at home to have a line of furry spaniels of various shapes, sizes and colours, all sitting in a row with their feed bowls on the ground about a metre in front of them, waiting for the moment to charge in and eat up. But the best thing about it is that this

▶ *The feed bowl routine helps keep the pup obedient all through his life*

instruction, once learnt with the feed bowl, then works in every situation where you want your dog to sit.

Try it with one of his toys. Hold it above pup's head just like the feed bowl, and say 'sit' and you will find pup sits. You can very quickly reach the point where you can place the toy down, or hide it, and keep pup sitting until you let him go to find his toy. Or, and here comes the clever bit, if there are times when you want him to sit still for a minute while you answer the door or pour the kettle or whatever, you can tell him to sit, and that's exactly what he will do. This can be very useful at times!

Many inexperienced people are quite critical of the whole idea of dog training. They might say that you are 'teasing' the dog by not giving food immediately, or ask what's the point of having a dog that will sit quietly when asked to do so? We'll be discussing this in more detail in Part Two, which explores the theory of dog owning and training, but I think that once you have discovered this very simple instruction and how useful it is, you and puppy will be quite keen on the whole idea. You already have a young puppy who comes to you when you call hisname, and now he also sits when you ask him to. These two instructions: 'come' and 'sit' are the foundation stones for having a well-behaved dog. Everything you do in the future, whether it's a walk in the park or search and rescue work, is just an extension of these two basics. And if you are consistent in teaching them at this early stage, you will have a pup who understands and cooperates even as young as three months old – and, of course, for the rest of his life.

If you have a particularly wriggly, supple and athletic breed of dog, you are likely to encounter a small problem with the early stages of the feed bowl sit. When I started using the technique to train cocker spaniel puppies I was disheartened to discover they were more than capable of looking up at the feed bowl without their bums automatically hitting the floor – no matter how high I attempted to hold up the bowl, and I am not very tall! They are also not a breed that is particularly greedy, so the feed bowl isn't quite the magnet it would be for a terrier or a retriever. At first I couldn't see how I was going to get anywhere. Some trainers recommend physically pushing pup into sitting position, but that contradicted the kind of seamless, instinctive training I wanted to achieve. But in a couple of days I noticed that when Tara (my first pup) was really concentrating and paying attention to me, she would naturally sit down, even if only for a second or so. So I developed a technique of using Tara's favourite toy. I would say her name and show her the toy, and as she came steaming over to get it, I would quickly raise it up out of her reach. I found that at that point she usually skidded into a sitting position, if only briefly. That was when I seized the moment to say 'hup' and give the toy as a reward. She caught on very quickly and I was soon able to introduce the feed bowl method as well.

So don't be afraid to experiment a little and find out what works with your pup. Don't overdo the 'sit' lesson, and always reward. Don't tell puppy off for not sitting, as ninety-nine times out of a hundred, the reason they haven't sat is because they don't understand what you want them to do. Equally, don't go on repeating the instruction over and over again when you are clearly not getting anywhere. Part Two of the book discusses the reasoning behind this. For the moment, while pup is still so young, just go with the flow. If it doesn't work the first time, wait till next feed time and try again. Be patient and positive and you will be surprised how quickly it does happen.

Yes and no

The only other important lesson for the young pup is learning the difference between 'yes' and 'no'; between right and wrong; between good and bad; between nice and naughty. It's as fundamental for a puppy as it is for a child. So basic really, that you can't call it a lesson; it's just the way your puppy's life is going to be as he grows up. Part Two contains a detailed discussion of why this is so important, and the theory behind it. But for these first few weeks of puppy owning, it is helpful to have some basic emergency tips about what to do.

The good news is that you don't need to do much. In fact with some pups you hardly need to do anything at all; they just seem to be born good. Fizz was very charming as a little pup and I can't remember ever having to tell her off at all. She is very bright and caught on quickly to each new situation, which I think made it easier for her to be good. Even so, all pups will start pushing the boundaries at some stage. Remember though, that a lot of what seems like naughtiness is in fact part of the puppy's development and learning. The way they discover that if you jump into the kitchen sink you may break crockery is by jumping into the kitchen sink and breaking crockery. So don't be too quick to push the angry button. Cut the pup some slack and try to avoid the worst disasters by prevention.

For most pups, your voice is all the correction you will ever need. Dogs are hugely responsive to vocalisation, whether from other dogs or from humans, and they instinctively distinguish between praising and cross tones of voice. A marked difference between your happy, praising voice and your angry, forbidding voice, is important. If you want to tell pup off for nipping your ankle, you must do so in a gruff tone of voice, not in a nice way. A lot of dog owners – even very experienced ones – make the mistake of saying things like: 'aah, what a naughty little boy' in a cute-let's-cuddle voice, which sends a really mixed message to the pup. Is he being naughty or not? Is the boss pleased or angry? Of course, you have to make your own mind up as well, and definitely be one or the other, which will be discussed in depth in Part Two.

So if pup has done something you don't want him to do, just say very sharply: 'Aach, aach, NO' and the pup will quickly get the message. It's unlikely you will ever have to do any more than that. But if you have a very bold, boisterous pup who is persisting, just grab him by the scruff of his neck and pick him up so that both front paws are off the floor. This imitates what his mother would do and lets him know firmly who is in control of the situation. It works equally well for larger or smaller breeds of dog.

If pup is doing what you want him to do, always remember to praise him. I was in a hospital waiting room the other day, with of course nothing to do but people-watch, and an awful lot of time to do it in. Mum and Dad and small daughter were also waiting, and small daughter was playing very happily and nicely with the various toy oddments that the hospital had managed to provide. Occasionally she would toddle over to Mum or Dad to show them what she had made or done with the toys. Unfortunately Mum and Dad were in the middle of one of those whispered rows we all end up having from time to time, and they were too busy to notice their daughter. I made a small bet with myself that very soon the child would stop playing nicely and start being naughty, which happened in due course. At which point Mum immediately broke off from the row and rounded-up her daughter to tell her off. But the daughter still went on being naughty, and getting told off.

Mum and Dad hadn't taken any notice of her good behaviour, and so their daughter hadn't been rewarded for it. The daughter wanted attention though, and soon discovered a way of getting attention from her parents. Even though Mum was telling her daughter off, she was giving her attention all the same – and therefore rewarding her bad behaviour, rather than her good behaviour. So Mum and Dad were unintentionally training their daughter to be a naughty girl.

Substitute puppy for daughter, and this is exactly how naughty dogs are made. Part Two will discuss your role as your puppy's boss in more detail, but for now all you need to remember is: reward good behaviour. Do it every time, and you will rarely encounter bad behaviour.

PUPPY'S KEY STAGE ONE: 12 weeks/3 months

This is a simple check list to make sure everything is going to plan by the time puppy has reached approximately three months old.

- Has been wormed and vaccinated

- Eats regularly with a good appetite

- Has regular bowel movements neither too loose nor too firm

- Knows his name and responds to it

- Is toilet trained

- Has regular rest and sleep

- Sits when asked

- Waits to be told before eating his food

- Plays happily with his toys without being possessive

Q. How long will toilet training take?

A. The more effort you put in, the less time it will take. If puppy basically never gets a chance to go to the loo in the wrong place, you will achieve it more or less straight away. If you are lazy, haphazard or very busy with other things it will take longer, but you will get there in the end. Pups prefer to go to the loo in the right place given a chance.

Q. Isn't it cruel to leave my puppy shut into his pen?

A. Your puppy's pen is the equivalent of your child having her own bedroom. It is somewhere for him to feel secure, that is his own base, where he can chill out without having to think about everything going on in the world round him. But don't use the pen as an excuse to ignore your puppy. He needs it for sleeping and relaxing, but not more than that.

Q. Do I really need to bother with worming and vaccination – the vet seems very expensive?

A. If you don't vaccinate your dog you won't be able to take him out and about as he won't be immune from canine distemper ('hard pad'); canine parvovirus; infectious canine hepatitis; kennel cough; and leptospirosis. Worming is essential to protect not just your dog but the whole family. And a good relationship with your vet will help you on many levels, including plenty of free advice on management, socialisation and training.

Q. The breed I like is quite expensive, but I have seen a cheap pup online. Should I buy it?

A. This really isn't recommended, especially for your first puppy. The cost of a puppy should always be a reflection of the true cost of breeding it. Fashionable breeds and toy breeds are often very expensive, but this is largely because they are expensive to breed. They don't have many pups in a litter, and often have birthing problems leading to big vet's bills. The cost of the stud dog is also high. So if you see a pup from one of those breeds advertised cheaply, you can be sure someone is cutting corners somewhere, which could lead to problems for you if you buy the pup.

Q. How do I know if I am feeding the pup enough?

A. Your vet will give you guidance on this at the puppy check. Generally, you should expect your pup to be growing quite fast at the same time as remaining a little bit chubby. He will go through phases of looking a bit gangly and disconnected as he grows, but you shouldn't be able to see hip bones. If he starts leaving food, that's a sign that you (or someone else in the family!) is overfeeding him. Once he is settled in he should always polish off his bowlful at one sitting. Don't feed titbits as they will upset his digestion and make his appetite irregular.

Q. I have been told I need to be dominant over the pup. How should I do that?

A. Don't bother about this! There is a huge amount of nonsense talked about so-called 'dominance' and Part Two has a thorough discussion of this issue if you want to find out more. A reader once asked me about his difficulty establishing 'dominance' over the new puppy – which turned out to be a three-month-old cocker pup small enough to sit in your hand! Definitely a case of 'pick on someone your own size'.

Q. Why is my puppy reluctant to come to me?

A. Young puppies are sometimes quite shy, particularly if their breeder's home was quiet. If you are quite a big, outgoing person or your family is quite boisterous, it can be a bit much for pup. Also if lots of family members are trying to play with him at the same time, it can all get a bit stressful and confusing. So make yourself small and quiet, and take it in turns to play with pup. At the opposite end of the spectrum, a confident, rufty-tufty pup can sometimes start playing games with you. If they have a favourite toy or something to investigate, they may prefer to do that than come to you. So get hold of their toy and they will soon come to play with it – and with you. You need to engage the pup's attention and be the most interesting thing in the room/garden. A good trick is to crawl up to him and gently get his scruff and drag him toward you. Or you could run away from him. Or even jump up and down making strange noises! You might want to explain this to the neighbours or the rest of the family before you try it.

Q. How much exercise/training should I give my pup?

A. This varies somewhat depending on the breed, and your vet or breed society will be able to give specific advice, but generally young pups need almost no formal exercise. The general exercise they get from playing in the garden and on their lavatory breaks should be plenty for the first few months. It is the same with training. At this stage the puppy is learning very quickly about the world in general, and that is plenty to keep his brain occupied. Make his play learning-centred, and just concentrate on coming to his name and sitting for the feed bowl as outlined above. There's no need to do anything else in these early weeks.

Q. How should I punish my pup?

A. I am hoping that if you stick carefully to the step-by-step survival guide as outlined, you won't need to punish your pup. In fact one of the big aims of this whole book is that you will never have to punish your pup – not now, and certainly not when he's perfect! The nearest my grown-up dogs at home ever come to being punished is being made to walk to heel rather than crashing headlong into the vegetable patch. Part Two will discuss in detail the whole question of discipline and how to establish it without using punishment.

However, you do need to teach your pup right from wrong. It is very simple. When he is being good praise him verbally and give him a cuddle. When he is bad, say: 'Aach, aach, NO' in a firm, brisk voice and walk away from him. A pup that is destined for greatness, perhaps with a career ahead of him as a competition or search and rescue dog, will often have a high level of intelligence and motivation, which we call 'drive'. Pups with a lot of drive do push the boundaries from time to time. If that happens, I just pick the pup up by the scruff of the neck and say: 'Oy, NO'. Even large breed pups are still small enough for you to do this at this stage – and this is the time to do it, when the lesson is easily learnt and rarely has to be repeated.

Never punish your pup until you understand his personality and are absolutely sure he is deliberately being naughty. Check out Part Two for how to interpret your pup's behaviour.

Q. My pup is a bit snappy. What should I do?

A. First of all, relax! Some breeds are more prone to nip than others. If you are lucky enough to have a Labrador retriever pup (the most popular pedigree dog in both the UK and the USA) it is easy to be a bit dismissive of people who are anxious or even a little bit intimidated about their pup biting. A reader wrote to tell me: 'My pup is biting when I reach in to drag him out of his pen. Will I need to have him put down?' Stay calm, keep your common sense. For example if that pup is biting when you reach in and drag him out of his pen – don't reach in and drag him out of his pen! Open the pen and call him to come out. If he is reluctant to come out, you need to think about why that might be – and this canine psychology area is something we will cover in detail in Part Two.

There are different kinds of snapping and nipping.

The defensive reflex is for the pup to bite when in pain or frightened. So check that you are holding the pup correctly and not causing him any pain in the way that you pick him up. Or has he an injury you haven't noticed? With almost all domestic animals, pain is the number one cause of difficult behaviour. Is your pup frightened? If he is showing other symptoms of fear like hiding, cowering, wetting himself, turning on his back, then you need to think about why he might be scared and how to reassure him.

Exploration and learning is another major reason for a puppy to mouth you and other objects. In just the way that babies put everything in their mouths, so do pups – and that may mean migrating from your shoe laces to your ankles. If you don't want tiny teeth marks, just reach down and pick up puppy by the scruff and say firmly: 'NO'. Do this every time and they will soon give up. Or you can consider it charming and spend the next ten years apologising to visitors for the fact that your dog is an ankle biter.

Breed temperament does play a part as well. Often breeds that were used for herding, fighting or vermin control originally are more prone to grow up to nip or even bite. For example, some people take the view that it is acceptable for a terrier to nip people's ankles. Then they let the terrier up on the sofa and are surprised when it bites someone's nose. No sort of nipping is acceptable at any stage or age or by any breed – end of. We will explore special breed issues elsewhere, but while the pup is so young, it is easy to nip nipping in the bud. Firstly, don't allow yourself to be intimidated or worried. You are older, wiser and bigger than this little pup. All he needs is firm guidance from you, which means picking him up by the scruff of the neck and firmly saying 'NO' every single time he tries a nip.

PUPPY FIRST AID KIT

Just in case, it is a good idea to have a first aid kit in the cupboard, ready for any emergency that might happen throughout your dog's life. Here's what to include:

• Saline solution in squeezy bottle – simplest to buy a commercial preparation aimed at contact lens wearers. This is used for rinsing any little scrapes or grazes. Anything more serious should be seen by the vet.

• Barrier cream – the kind of thing you use for nappy/diaper rash is fine. Puppies sometimes get sore or spotty underparts from rushing around in the undergrowth and the barrier cream helps prevent and treat this.

• Old-fashioned eye dropper or empty squeezy water bottle – this is very useful if for any reason you need to rehydrate your pup or dog in a hurry and he is not drinking. My dim-witted but lovely dog Dutch once made himself so ill eating windfalls that he got dehydrated and I was able to bring him round by squirting a rehydration mixture straight into his mouth. Do get the dog to the vet though if the dog is showing signs of shock (pale gums, flicking eyes, shivering).

• Ear cleansing drops – available from pet shops or the vet, very useful for grooming and breeds prone to wax.

• **Eye rinse drops** – from pet shops or vets, useful for washing out grass seeds for example.

• **Cotton wool** – for general cleaning, padding, etc.

• **Cohesive bandage** – a stretchy bandage that sticks to itself and has lots of general uses.

• **Rice Pudding** – normal pre-made tin will keep for ages and has magical properties for a pup with an upset tum or poor appetite.

PART ONE: SUMMARY

STEP-BY-STEP SURVIVAL GUIDE UP TO TWELVE WEEKS OLD

Now you've had your puppy for just a month or so, but already you and he have learnt so much. Here's a quick reminder of the things covered in this section.

PAW (Puppy Arrival Week) minus 2 weeks: speak to breeder; get puppy kit together; establish a puppy pen; puppy-proof the house.
PAW minus 1 week: book vet appointment; consider insurance; plan the pick-up; prepare the car.
PAD (Puppy Arrival Day): set out early; remember to pick up puppy pack as well as pup; teach children to pick up and hold puppy; first house-training moments; first feed; leave pup to rest.
Weeks 1 and 2: routines for feed, house-training, sleeping; vet's appointment; teach puppy his name; toys and play.
Weeks 3 and 4: grooming; the feed bowl lesson; right and wrong.
Puppy's Key Stage One
Frequently Asked Questions
First Aid

Now you're through the first frantic few weeks, there's time to think more about training and owning your pup. Part Two will tell you all you need to know to be a Perfect Puppy Owner, looking at the thinking behind what we do when living with our dogs.

PART TWO

HOW TO BE A PERFECT PUPPY OWNER

Now that the frantic first few weeks have been successfully managed, there's time to think about what happens next. This section is going to help you find out what is ahead of you as you get to know dogs. It is all about training you, so that you will find it easier to train your dog. You will discover how to be the perfect puppy owner – not quite the same as being the owner of a perfect puppy! By the end of the book, you will have achieved both. If this is the family's first dog, you and the puppy are both going to learn together. This section will give you an idea of what to expect – and what your puppy will expect.

▶ *My cocker spaniel puppy, Fizz, at six months – an energetic, fast-maturing breed*

DOs and DON'Ts of Puppy Ownership

DO respect your pup as a fellow living creature

DO be consistent in your behaviour

DO establish a good routine

DO take responsibility for the pup's upbringing

DO understand your own shortcomings

DON'T neglect your puppy

DON'T let your puppy run wild

DON'T lose your temper

DON'T spoil your puppy or treat him like a human

DON'T allow bad behaviour in public

What is a dog?

This may sound a strange question to ask. Surely we all know what a dog is! But getting the answer to this question right is fundamental to your future relationship with your dog. If you know what your dog really is, you will know a lot about him and you will get along together better as a result. And yet we seem to get the answer to this question wrong very often and in lots of different ways. First of all, most of us – and I am as guilty of this as anyone – have a big tendency to think of a dog as just a furry human being. This is understandable, because in fact the puppy's early needs are very similar to those of a human baby. They both need regular small feeds and plenty of attention, monitoring and physical affection. As they grow up they benefit from a regular routine and they both need some form of potty/house-training. Young puppies often behave in a very similar way to babies – putting their heads on one side, nuzzling and generally 'being cute'. Both have the kind of big eyes and soft features that encourage our tender feelings.

So it is very easy to get off on the wrong paw by starting to think of your pup as being more human than he actually is. But your pup will very quickly become a full-grown dog. At eight months old he is an adolescent, and most breeds are more or less fully physically mature at around eighteen months old. By this point you need to understand what a dog is not, and the answer is that he is not a human being, and certainly not a baby. It is equally important that the dog should also know he is not a human being. The most common cause of behaviour problems in adult dogs is that the dog has been treated as a human to such an extent that he is not aware of any difference between himself and humans. This gives rise to all sorts of difficulties in recognising boundaries; in attitude to humans outside his immediate 'family'; and in interacting with other dogs (who do know they are dogs).

▶ *My cocker spaniel puppy, Fizz, at six months*

What do dogs think they are?

If you could ask a wild dog, or even a modern working dog, what he thinks he is, he would tell you that first and foremost he is a member of a pack. Pretty much everything else – number of paws, fur, etc. – is irrelevant to a dog compared with the importance of his pack and the *pack imperative*. The pack imperative is what enables a dog to survive in the wild. It gives him food to share; it protects him from predators; it gives him warmth and a den; eventually it may allow him to reproduce his own genes. If a puppy or young dog doesn't get it right with the pack, his chances of enjoying a happy old age are very low. So a puppy will very quickly learn his place in the hierarchy of the pack, and he will work out what are the right things to do to make sure he is generally acceptable to the pack. An intelligent pup will even learn ways to manipulate the pack to give himself a better position within the structure, and a pup that is both intelligent and strong may very well manage to get into a leadership role at the head of the pack.

Despite thousands of years of domestication, most modern dogs are still ruled by the pack imperative. And their pack imperative behaviour has many similarities with human social interaction. The kind of thing they have to do to make sure they are well in with the pack – like knowing when to be submissive, or bringing gifts of food or scavengings to other pack members – is similar to the things that humans do in order to be liked. Just like humans, some dogs are better at being popular than other dogs. Dogs who don't have a very good position within the pack may well exhibit a lot of insecurity and submissive behaviour, in just the way that anxious humans do. Dogs who are high up in the pack structure tend to be self-confident, rather like the school rugby captain. So it is all too easy to slip into the attitude that a dog really is thinking like a human – to anthropomorphise his behaviour.

Now comes the contradiction. On the one hand, it isn't a good idea to anthropomorphise dogs or animals in general. But, when it comes to bringing up and educating our pup to be a perfect mature dog, we are going to use his human-like pack imperative behaviours to help us with the training. Scientists and expert animal trainers call this 'behaviour modification'. We can interpret and use his pack imperative behaviours to communicate with him and to lead him to act the way we want him to. So what does all this mean for us as perfect puppy owners? Basically, we're going to understand puppy a little bit in human terms, but mainly, we're going to be more dog!

THE CANINE CONTRACT

As President Kennedy might have said, ask not what your dog can do for you, but what you can do for your dog. Owning a dog is a two-way relationship. You are going to get a lot from your dog, but you also have a responsibility to commit to your dog. I call this the Canine Contract.

Here's what you will be getting, or hoping to get, from your dog:

- **Companionship** – this is the primary reason dog owners all over the world give for having their dog.

- **Leisure enjoyment** – many research projects worldwide have shown that dog owners are less likely to suffer health problems. This is because the dog becomes a leisure activity, involving the owner in walking and often many other hobbies.

- **Love** – It is hardwired into a dog's DNA to bond with the person who looks after him. Dogs have no word for this relationship, but humans tend to call it love or loyalty, and it is tremendously reassuring as a human to be on the receiving end of it, even if only from your four-legged friend!

- **Protection** – guarding flocks and dwellings was almost certainly the primary reason mankind domesticated the dog in the first place, and many dogs still do this for a living – but even a pet dog will be protective of you and the family.

- **Commitment/obedience** – puppies are instinctively cooperative with training due to the pack imperative, and will continue to respond well as adult dogs, as long as they are treated properly.

- **Relaxation** – Many studies have shown that dog owners are less likely to suffer from stress-related illnesses and more able to deal with difficult life events. The therapeutic effects of interacting with dogs are now so well known that dogs are brought into hospitals to work with patients of all ages. In America, and increasingly in Britain, dogs are used to help young children feel safe enough to give evidence in court cases, by telling the dog the story rather than an adult.

• **Structure** – A dog needs to be fed and exercised in a regular routine. This does impose a structure on the life of the dog's owner, and for many different reasons, individuals and families often find it helpful to have a positive, regular framework underlying daily life.

• **Working assistance** – We've all heard of guide dogs, and there is a whole host of dogs out there working on our behalf as assistance dogs; sniffers; search and rescuers; medical detection dogs; farm dogs and country sports workers.

Here's what your dog should be able to expect from you:

• **Care and well-being** – Our fundamental duty as dog owners is, of course, to look after our dogs properly. Fortunately nearly everybody lucky enough to have a dog finds this to be completely obvious. If you've bothered to buy a book, you clearly care! Sadly though, there are parts of the world, and even certain groups of people in Britain and America, who do not recognise that dogs have a basic right to well-being and dignity. With your own dog, you don't need me to remind you to house, feed, water, worm, groom, exercise and interact with your dog. I also like to try and do my bit for other dogs worldwide, who aren't lucky enough to have me as their servant, by researching and donating to canine charities. For more details on how to do this, check out the back of the book.

• **Health** – Your puppy is dependent on you to keep him healthy. Annual boosters and a check-up are basic. It's also important not to let your dog get too fat or too thin. Make sure his coat is in good condition and he has no fleas or parasites. His eyes, ears and paws need to be checked regularly for infections, especially those caused by foreign bodies like grass seeds. Keep his teeth clean and his gums healthy, otherwise it will be a problem in old age.

• **Freedom** – Not many dog owners really give this much thought. We tend to assume that if we are going about our own lives freely, so is the dog. But from the dog's point of view this may not always be the case. For example, a dog who spends his entire life on a lead because he has not been taught basic

▲ *If you are confident your dogs will come when you call, they can enjoy a lot more freedom*

obedience, is not as free as a dog who can be allowed to roam because his owner is confident he will return when asked. Try to think clearly about the life and routine your dog will have with you over the years, and work out how free that life will really be from the dog's point of view.

• **Companionship** – Just as we look to our dogs for companionship, they too need the reassuring contact of a fellow 'pack member'. The dog relies on you to provide this. Don't just offer him companionship when you need it and then leave him high and dry while you are busy. Leaving a dog all alone for long hours is emotionally painful for a pack animal. If you are not going to be

▶ *It is worth considering two dogs to keep each other company*

around much, to make provision for your dog to get companionship from dog-walkers, sitters, neighbours or, if possible, another dog is the best solution.

● **Commitment** – The phrase: 'A dog is for life, not just for Christmas,' has become famous since it was first used by The Dogs Trust in a campaign in Britain. As you have bothered to buy and read a book all about your puppy, it is obvious that you have already signed up to the commitment pledge – well done!

● **Respect** – This is an aspect of our relationship with our dogs that is rather more complex than you might think. Most of us would agree that we like to be respected by our work colleagues, friends and hopefully our family – and we would probably include the dog in that. But respect is a two-way street and often the best way to earn it is by showing it yourself. So respect what your dog is, and be responsive to what his needs genuinely are, as opposed to what you might think he wants. Is it respectful to your dog to put him in a diamante dog jacket to match your handbag? For some breeds of dog, the answer to this question may well be yes! Having watched toy dogs, especially at the annual 'Dog Day' party in London's Chelsea, I have come to the conclusion that many lap dogs really do enjoy being dressed up and taken around town. That doesn't alter the fact that my own rufty-tufty spaniels would hate it. So be sensitive about your dog's reactions to this kind of thing and respect them.

● **Protection** – Once upon a time they protected our homes and farms, and now our family dogs need us to protect them. Bear in mind the dangers of theft, traffic and other dogs. Remember that the most simple things can be dangerous, for example slug pellets which are toxic to dogs if they eat too many. Even a half-frozen pond can spell disaster.

- Fulfilment – I've left this until last because it is probably one of the most difficult aspects of your dog's life to evaluate, and I really wouldn't blame anyone who doesn't take this on board. The saying is 'every dog has his day' and you have to ask yourself: am I giving my dog the opportunity to have his day? Has he genuinely had the chance to achieve all he is capable of doing, or is he just sitting around bored and chewing the carpet in frustration? So many readers come to me with problems with their working breed puppy (especially collies and gundogs), complaining that the dog is always getting into trouble and being destructive or even chasing sheep. These highly intelligent breeds need to keep their brains occupied, and if you don't keep them busy, they will find their own amusements. So if you have a special pup, consider some of the activities like agility, search and rescue or obedience which are discussed in Part Five of the book. Can you honestly say your dog is going to be the best a dog can be?

Sign up to the Canine Contract now, and your puppy will be only too happy to add his paw print!

Training the family first

All of us brought up on a diet of children's adventure books and Disney movies probably have an image of the ideal family of Mum, Dad, brother and sister, and, of course, the dog, Topper. It is ideal too – but only if Topper is a lovely chap who can be relied on not to bite or bark or chase. And only if the kids are nice to him and remember to take him on his walks and groom him. So if you have chosen to get a puppy as a wonderfully positive thing for your young family, that's a great idea, especially if you get your children involved from the beginning and teach them along with the puppy.

However, the family will need a few lessons, and maybe even some rules. With older children, get them learning how to look after pup along with you. Hopefully they will enjoy this book. There is a section at the back for your children to create their own **Dog Log** and put it online. Lots of teenagers I know have blogs for their dogs and many dogs even have their own web page. I'm embarrassed to admit that my dog, Ginger (aka FTCh Gournaycourt Ginger), has more images and entries on Google than I do! Having a dog log and an online presence for your dog is also very useful just in case the worst happens and he strays or gets stolen.

Very young children won't be able to get quite so involved, but there's no harm in them being hands-on (literally) while you or their brothers and sisters keep an eye out. Remember though, don't leave a young child alone with either an adult dog or a puppy. Children and dogs can both be unpredictable sometimes, and if one or the other manages to frighten or confuse the other one the results can be disastrous, even with otherwise placid dogs or children.

A 'family dog' should be just that, a dog for all the family to enjoy and look after. However it's not always an easy thing to manage. There are many pitfalls. Who is the person who is ultimately responsible for looking after the dog? Who is the person training the dog? Will everybody take turns remembering to exercise or feed or groom the dog? What happens if someone forgets their turn? What happens if different members of the family are teaching the dog different verbal instructions? Suppose somebody is deliberately jazzing the dog up just to wind up another member of the family – it does happen!

So there do need to be rules, or maybe as Captain Jack Sparrow's Pirate Code would put it: 'guidelines'. It's not vital exactly what your guidelines are, but they must be absolutely clear, and everybody should know them and try to stick to them as far as possible (at least as far as a pirate would!). Here's what your dog code needs to cover:

Who is the officer-in-command of the dog? This is by far the most important thing to get sorted out from the start. Basically it is true that 'a dog can only have one master'. One person (probably you) must be the boss. The dog's boss has the last word on what happens with the dog, including training and also has the ultimate responsibility for the dog's welfare. Not having a dog boss leads to all sorts of family conflicts as everybody blames each other for Topper getting into trouble again.

Who will feed and exercise the dog? On a daily basis? At weekends/ occasionally? Try and divide this up among family members; it is good for children to have minor responsibilities. But make sure everybody knows exactly what they are signed up for.

Is there a rota for basic dog duties (including grooming, etc.)? It doesn't have to be anything so formal as a chart stuck on the fridge. But whoever is the dog boss should have an idea in their mind of who they want to help them with the dog from time to time. Your teenage daughter may be far too tied up with studying during the week, but might end up enjoying a breezy walk with Topper at the weekend – despite initial reluctance! Definitely don't get left being the only one who ever does these things, especially if you are then going to get chippy about it.

Who is in charge of dog training? Again, this is usually the dog boss, though not always, if perhaps you have an enthusiastic teenager who's keen to learn about dog training. The main thing is that the dog boss must have the last word when it comes to training. Never let your children all be yelling at the puppy with loads of different instructions. If two or three people are calling puppy from different parts of the garden, he can't win. He can only go to one person at a time, and therefore he's disobeyed the other two. So it is very confusing and stressful for the pup. Nor should children be allowed to play with the pup endlessly. The pup will end up mentally and physically exhausted and will either switch off completely or even become snappy and aggressive.

Who is in the officer's seat? When we had our first puppy, my husband and I used to enjoy going on lovely country walks with her, which often ended up becoming somewhat romantic. Tara soon discovered that when Hugh and I were distracted, she could bomb off somewhere. At first this led to minor rows as we blamed each other for letting her out of sight. At about the same time, I started training her onto a whistle, and we discovered the answer. Whoever was wearing the whistle round their neck had ultimate responsibility for Tara at that point, rather like being officer of the watch. Whenever I was wearing the whistle I would refuse all romantic advances so that I could concentrate on my duty to watch Tara. Whenever Hugh was wearing the whistle he would put Tara on the lead and tie her to a tree if he was about to be distracted. You see how dogs teach you about humans as well as canines!

Establishing routines

When it comes to bringing up your puppy to be a credit to you, routine is the best helper you have. You will already have discovered how helpful routine is when it comes to toilet training. Routine also helps the puppy and young dog to be more settled, relaxed and obedient in his daily life. Dogs definitely have an internal body clock, just as we do. And experiments have shown that they also seem to be able to keep count of days. Where a routine event happens just once a week, rather than daily, dogs seem to know which day to expect it. Scientists are still not quite sure how this happens. Some suggest that the dogs are not counting days at all, but are simply picking up cues from our body language that a particular event is about to happen. However other experiments have taken the human element out of the equation and still found the dogs were able to predict accurately when a routine event was about to happen. It may be that this talent was originally helpful to dogs in the wild in order to follow the movement patterns of their prey.

Whatever the reason, it is certainly very useful to us in training. At one level it's just a bit of fun when a young dog knows it is time for his walk and goes and brings you his lead. But in animal behaviour terms it means you are pushing on an open door when you ask a dog to do something, if he was already expecting to do it in any case. My dogs have their breakfast after their walk each morning. It is fascinating to see that, no matter where we have been walking, as we approach home they will automatically finish their walk and go and sit beside their kennels and wait for me. It's also extremely useful to have them all present and correct if I have been distracted by the postman or chatting to a neighbour. When I was doing the early obedience training with Fizz I used to take her to a different place from the everyday 'fun' walks, and she learnt very quickly that the routine of getting into the back of the 4x4 without any of the other dogs meant a lesson. By the time we arrived at the training ground she had her 'school day' head on and was a completely different animal from the joyful nutter running round with the other dogs at playtime.

So having a workable routine and sticking to it is very helpful. Get the routine right and you will get the dog right. But be careful that it is not the dog setting the routine. If he's always scratching at the door at 4.30 in the morning, this is probably not a routine you want to encourage! One of my early dog training failures, dear old Dutch (aka the world's worst gundog), established a routine that suited him very well. Every Tuesday was bin day, and of course the village bins would all be out in the lane ready for the bin men. So on a Tuesday morning, Dutch would give you the slip and be off down the lane to ransack the bins for unsavoury morsels. He only did this on Tuesdays. Either he could count, as we discussed, or more likely he could smell the exquisitely pungent odour of five-day-old sandwich wrapper! A dog sitter came to look after the dogs while we were away and we warned him about Tuesdays. But of course, when nothing happened on Sunday or Monday, the dog sitter was lulled into a false sense of security and assumed we were just useless dog owners (not far wrong). Then came Tuesday, and of course Dutch was off like a shot! The dog sitter was brave enough to confess that it took him hours to find Dutch and extract him from a particularly juicy black bag.

Routines need to be the right routines, and they need to be your routines. Don't try to rush into setting a routine. Just see what works for you over the first couple of months and then let that develop into a routine that is hassle-free and workable in the long term.

Think dog, talk dog

When I started out with training on gundogs, the top professional trainers told me: 'You need to be two steps ahead of your dog.' They meant that I needed to be able to anticipate the dog's every move, and often know what a dog is about to do before the dog himself has entirely made up his mind. This is quite a difficult skill to develop, but well worth it. It involves not just reading the dog's body language, but actually thinking like a dog. So how does a dog think? Nobody really knows. For example, obviously we know dogs can't talk, and it is fairly clear they don't think in words the way we do. Yet even a fairly average dog is capable of learning a vocabulary of at least twelve human verbal instructions. My dogs for example, appear to understand the meanings of the words or phrases: 'come'; 'hup/sit'; 'stay'; 'get busy'; 'get on'; 'get out'; 'go back'; 'leave'; 'drop'; 'steady'; 'no'; 'good'; 'bad'; 'in'; 'kennel'; 'bed'; 'heel'; 'lost/seek'; 'bring'; and of course their names. I don't for a minute think that they assign meanings to these words in the way that a human would. I don't think they even trigger a thought process.

From long observation, I think it is more likely that a dog responds to a word through association rather than thought process – this is certainly the case with a well-trained dog. If you say 'sit down' to a human child, she will understand what the words mean, and have a thought process something like this: 'Mummy has asked me to sit down. That is what she wants me to do. Is that what I want to do? If yes, then fine I will sit down. If not, then I need to think about what to do next.'

If you say 'sit' to a dog, it hears 'sssssiiT', a specific shape and type of sound which it associates with its bum hitting the ground. If you have trained your dog well, that's all there is to it. The sound and the action of bum hitting ground amount to the same thing, without any intervening thought process. If you haven't trained the dog properly, it will be only vaguely familiar with the sound of the word 'sssssiiT'. It may not have any actions associated with that sound or it may be very confused. So it either won't do anything or it may do the wrong thing, or it may come running up to you. There is also another outcome with highly intelligent dogs, who have 'drive' and usually end up being highly trained for specific work. These dogs recognise the sound of the word and have the association, but sometimes they appear to make a decision about whether to follow the association or not.

I had a very successful dog called Lyn who was very intelligent and won lots of competitions. One day my husband was out walking her. He'd allowed her to go off hunting around further away than she was really meant to, so he called her back. At the same moment, a rabbit whizzed past Lyn's nose – a huge temptation to go and chase it! He describes Lyn standing still and looking at him for a moment, and also glancing at the disappearing bunny. It was absolutely clear to him that she was judging the distance between him and her, and between her and the rabbit. You couldn't avoid seeing a thought process: 'Is Dad near enough to me to run up and tell me off before I can get going and chase this rabbit? No, not a chance. So I will run off.' Which she promptly did and was right, by the way, about my husband not being able to catch her! So even well-trained dogs can certainly make choices. There is definitely some kind of mental reasoning going on in their heads – but don't make the mistake of assuming it is verbal, or necessarily anything like our own thought process. I think in the case of Lyn it was more like: 'Umm, "come" sound from Dad, strong. Umm big, big lovely rabbit smell; rabbit smell stronger; go.'

The primary sense for dogs is their sense of smell. It is much, much stronger than the human sense of smell. Dogs can detect a cancer cell by its smell. Their noses have at least 125 million olfactory receptors for scent molecules that make them thousands of times more sensitive to smell than human beings. If a dog appears to be turning his head to look at something, it is much more likely that he is in fact turning his nose to sniff at something. So a smell is probably the strongest imperative, the clearest command, a dog gets. It is much more likely to obey and believe what he smells than the evidence of any other sense. Dog trainers who want their dogs to retrieve a particular item are often baffled when their dog won't pick up the object lying in full sight in front of them, but continues to hunt around 'looking' for it. The truth is that the dog is actually 'sniffing' for it rather than looking. Even if he can see the object, if he can't also smell it, the dog won't believe in the object.

You can use this knowledge when you are training your dog. If your dog is going to run off, he will almost always run off into the wind, where all the amazing smells are coming from. So when you are training your dog, or just taking him for a walk, check out the wind direction before you start. If there's trouble ahead, that's where it will come from! If you ever have to go looking for a dog, always start by searching into the wind from where he went missing, as that's the most likely direction he will have gone. For humans, smell is our least good sense, so it puts us at a disadvantage when trying to communicate with our dogs, because it's something we will never have in common. But by gaining an understanding of how smell works, we can at least understand some of its impact on dogs and therefore why they are behaving as they are.

It's not just smell. There are lots of areas where we need to 'think dog' in order to improve our relationship. For example, quite literally, a dog's point of view is different from ours because his eye level is so much lower than ours. Get down on your hands and knees so that your eyes are roughly at the same height as your dog's eye level. It's amazing how different everything looks. Long grass becomes an impenetrable jungle from the dog's point of view. His horizon is much closer, and small rises in the ground are impossible to see over. Sometimes, if your dog acts as if he can't see you, he really can't see you. Often dogs leap or stand on their hind legs like meerkats so that they can see over long grass or bumps.

So a dog lives in a completely different sensory world from ours, and if you can take this on board and understand his point of view, it will help tremendously in communicating with him. Watch your pup closely as he grows up and try to get your own 'puppy dictionary' of his body language and behaviours. There's much more about this in Part Three, when we start serious training of the young pup, but for now it's really helpful to understand what his particular gestures and actions mean. For example, as a pup, Fizz very helpfully had a habit of putting her head quizzically on one side when she was confused or puzzled by something. I noticed this, and when it came to training her, I could always tell if she really understood a lesson or not by whether she put her head on one side. That was her 'tell'.

There are lots of others. Belly-crawling can mean a pup is being submissive and not feeling confident enough to obey an instruction. But beware, some very clever dogs soon discover that you let up on them when they belly-crawl, so they do it to pretend they are sorry and encourage you to go easy on them. If you've ever read Charles Dickens's *David Copperfield* you will recognise the character of Uriah Heep and his catchphrase: 'I'm a 'umble person' – but Heep turned out to have an agenda that wasn't humble at all. It can take a while to discover if you have a 'Uriah Heep' dog. By being observant now, you won't be fooled so easily when the pup gets older.

All the time that you are getting an understanding of how to 'think dog', you are essentially learning his language, which means you will also be able to 'talk dog' when you need to. Your pup will also be trying to understand your language every bit as much as you are trying to understand his. The pack imperative means that it is very important for a young dog to keep a close eye on you and try and work out what you want and what you might do next. Many people describe their dogs as being more or less telepathic in their understanding of them. You often hear dog owners say: 'It's as if he knows what I'm thinking' or 'he seems to know what I'm going to do next.' In fact this is usually just because the dog is focusing on you intensely and studying you very carefully. Especially if he sees you as his pack leader, predicting your behaviour is every bit as important to him as it is for you to predict his behaviour.

Leadership

Let's face it, dogs are natural squaddies! They don't on the whole show a lot of initiative. Left to themselves, dogs are not particularly enterprising souls. Their biggest ambition is to retain ownership of their bone and have a comfortable spot to sleep in. Choices, decision making, long-term planning, strategic thinking, career goals – none of these things feature on their agenda for life. They would much rather you took care of that side of things. Just like a bunch of soldiers looking for a major, dogs say: 'We want you to be our officer.' All you need to do is work out what it takes to be a good officer. Of course if you do already have experience as an officer or similar leadership role with humans, so much the better. Dogs are much easier to command and control than humans!

Animal behaviourists tend to go on at length about 'dominance' and 'pack hierarchy', but the reality is much simpler. If you have good leadership skills already, you will find it easy to train your dog. Even if you haven't seen yourself as much of a leader up to now, your dog will look to you to be one, and you will almost certainly find yourself slotting into the role without difficulty. Many people find that through dog training they learn a lot of skills that are very useful elsewhere in life. Having just stepped down from a senior executive position on a national daily newspaper when I got my first puppy, I was certainly used to management and leadership already, but even so I have found that dog training has given me huge insights into how to handle all sorts of situations, not just canine. You discover when and how to be assertive and firm, and when to take the pressure off. You become particularly quick to spot developing problems and nip them in the bud.

Taking control of a situation is a particular talent that I find myself putting into practice with call centres! For example, when training your dog you will soon discover that threatening a dog is completely pointless. Either do or don't do. If you threaten but don't follow through, the dog immediately assumes that he has won. Instead you must make it absolutely clear to the dog what outcome it is that you want. If he fails to reach the outcome, you must demonstrate the consequences immediately. It is the same with a call centre! You should tell the operative exactly what it is you want to happen as a result of your conversation, and if that doesn't happen you must escalate the matter immediately. No losing your temper and threatening dire but vague consequences. Simply assert firmly what the outcome of the call will be, and you will find that is what happens.

Your puppy will love you for being assertive, clear and consistent in your leadership. It takes all the pressure off him. He doesn't have to second guess you all the time or find himself in unpredictable situations with you. It makes him feel secure and comfortable that you will always behave in the same way, and that makes him steady and reliable in turn.

Those of us who are not natural leaders will need to think a little about this issue. If you can't say boo to a goose, you are unlikely to be able to say boo to your dog. If your children are always running rings round you, it's probable that the dog will too. If you find it stressful to have junior colleagues depending on you at work, then your dog's needs will also be somewhat pressurising. But the good news is that learning how to train your dog is a great environment for improving your own self-confidence. It's nice to have a well-trained dog, but compared with bringing up a child or your career, it's very far from a deal-breaker. So it is a great non-pressurised opportunity to think about leadership without any great consequences if you find it problematic. Throughout this book you will be discovering that success in dog training requires you to have great leadership skills, and we'll discuss in detail how to develop them and put them into practice with your dog. The kind of officer qualities you will need are:

- **Confidence** – to be the boss of your dog and know that he will do as you ask at all times

- **Assertiveness** – to insist on what you want without being aggressive or bossy

- **Calmness** – not to panic when things go wrong but to respond as required to the situation

- **Clarity** – to know and express exactly what outcome you want in training and interacting with your dog

- **Patience** – to keep your temper when the dog is being dim and persist

- **Compassion** – to understand why things may be going wrong for your dog and to remain steadfast with him even when he disappoints you

- **Humour** – to defuse tension by being able to see the funny side

- **Consistency** – to behave the same way towards your dog no matter what is happening elsewhere in your life

- **Strategy** – to plan your training and overcome any difficulties

In your relationship with your dog, never forget that you are the officer and he is the private. It's obviously a bit of fun to think about it in this way, but it is also a very simple way of describing a real fundamental in dog training. You are not there to be a tyrant or to be aggressive and dominant over your dog, but you are there as a good officer to give him leadership and guide him into a positive future. And the dog must always be subordinate to you. A dog that has the idea he can be his own officer can quickly become a problem. These are the dogs that you find in total control of a family. These dogs create no-go areas within the home where the family dare not go because the dog has become territorial. Or they won't let guests into the house, or they display hyper-sexualised behaviour. Out on walks they may attack other dogs or knock over pushchairs. The owners are either too frightened to do anything, or they make excuses for the dog. The one I personally find irritating is: 'Oh, he's only playing' as a seven stone large breed dog cannons into a toddler and sends the child flying. These dogs are not playing; these dogs think they are in charge – and they are right.

Occasionally, particularly in working, assistance and competition-bred dogs, you do come across a pup that is genuinely officer material. Even when he was only six weeks old, Ginger used to collect all the bowls after feed time, stack them up and bring them to me to be washed – a useful habit he still performs to this day! He is a dog with a great sense of responsibility, and always looked after his litter sisters, to the point where they were rather overdependent on him. Sometimes when training him, I worried that I had set him too difficult a challenge, but he used to give me a reassuring look before going off to perform the task successfully. Sure enough, when it came to competitions he took it all in his stride and went on to win at the highest level and become a stud dog. But even so, Ginger was never officer-in-command. He was certainly my right-hand dog, but always a rank or two below. Where I was the major, he was the sergeant. Even when he knew more about a situation than I did, we always went through the motions of me being the one to give the commands – though I must admit he'd often already carried them out!

Reward and punishment

How – and whether – to reward and punish your dog is about the thorniest of all the issues in dog ownership. All the aspects of dog owning we've discussed so far all contribute a great deal to solving the issue of reward and punishment. If you are a good leader, your dog will be devoted to you. His best reward will be the knowledge that you are pleased with him, and just a sharp word or even a stern glance will be enough for him to realise you are disappointed with him. If you can think dog, you will never get into a situation where punishment is appropriate. If you have good routines, your dog is less likely to get in trouble with you; and the more your family is on-side, the easier it is to keep on a good path. So everything we have discussed so far comes together to create an environment where your dog never needs to be punished and his biggest reward is to share his life with you.

One of the softest dogs I have ever trained is Solo, who is four years old at the time of writing. Sadly he was the only puppy to survive from his litter, and his mum had a Caesarean, so he was mainly hand-reared. I can remember weighing him every day and the joy when he topped the 2lb mark. Of course, that has given him a special bond with me. I made sure he got integrated with the other dogs as soon as he was big enough, to make sure he grew up knowing he was a dog. He is now one of the happiest and bounciest of all in the current mob, to the extent that his nickname is Towser. Even so, just a glare from me is enough to bring him in to heel, and his best reward is getting a special cuddle from me.

The fashion among dog trainers today is not to talk about 'reward' and 'punishment' but about 'positive reinforcement' and 'negative reinforcement'. Both sets of phrases mean broadly the same thing, with a slight subtle difference. When we talk about 'reinforcement' we mean working with the dog's natural behaviours to achieve long-term training. So if the dog does what we want him to, whether by accident or in training, we quickly 'reinforce' this behaviour through praise and reward, which gives the dog the idea that what he just did is worth doing again. If the dog does something we don't want him to do, we don't react at all, leaving the dog with the feeling that to repeat his behaviour wouldn't get him anything. This is generally more successful and subtle than 'punishing' unwanted behaviour. Some dogs find the 'punishment' to be just another form of human interaction, which they want. So they may repeat the behaviour just to get the interaction, even though we as humans see it as a punishment. Tough dogs especially seem to have this view, and if you are not careful you can get locked into an escalating arms race of punishment. There are definitely some breeds (did I mention terriers?) who take the view: 'If you can't do the time, don't do the crime.' They know very well they can do the time, so on with the crime!

There will of course be occasions where you need to correct the dog, if he has misunderstood or is doing something incorrectly. Correction is different from punishment. For example, if your pup doesn't come when you call him, you will learn to go up to him and gently drag him in your direction. This is a correction. If your pup snaps at a visitor, you will pick him up by the scruff of the neck while telling him off verbally, and that is a punishment. The knack is to understand the difference between a failure to perform a training exercise – which requires correction – and actual misbehaviour which may occasionally need to be punished. It's a distinction which people often fail to make even when dealing with human situations. If a child gets his homework wrong, then it's a situation for help and correction. If a child refuses to do his homework, that might be a misbehaviour. Before rushing to punish, do ask yourself: is this pup deliberately misbehaving (rare) or has he simply got things a bit wrong? The latter is far more usual.

If there is an occasion where you really feel you must punish the dog, think carefully about what the punishment should be – and certainly never punish a dog if you are in a bad mood or have lost your temper. The punishment should not escalate the situation; nor should it be unintentionally rewarding; nor should it alienate the dog. Try to start with the minimum level of punishment, so that you still have somewhere to go if it continues to misbehave. If you've gone nuclear at the first moment, it doesn't leave you with many options. I don't use solitary confinement as a punishment because it alienates the dog and ultimately leaves him less humanised than before, which can be risky. Looking back over the dogs I've trained in the last few years, really all it has taken to get them back on the straight and narrow is a sharp 'aach, aach'. As I have a few dogs all living together, there is occasionally an outbreak of tetchiness between the dogs. If this happens, I go to the offending dog and roll him on his back, with my welly boot planted gently but firmly on his chest. This demonstrates to the dog in question that there is no point at all making a bid for dominance within the pack, as I am the leader. If a puppy is pushing the boundaries deliberately, I might pick him up by the scruff of the neck to let him realise what an insignificant little idiot he is. If a real problem is developing, it is much more important to break the cycle of offending behaviour through training rather than repeatedly punishing – and Parts Three and Four will discuss various training methods.

If you get your 'positive reinforcement' or 'reward', correct from the very beginning, it's unlikely you will ever need to bother about punishment.

Just as you thought about the right level of punishment, it's important to know what the right kind of 'positive reinforcement' is for your dog. This varies from breed to breed and can depend on what your dog will grow up to be. People with pet dogs, and obedience trainers, believe in using food as a reward. My dogs are all gundogs and food is not a particularly successful reward for them. It interferes with aspects of their training; leads to obesity in some gundog breeds; and really isn't that important to other gundog breeds. I'm lucky that my dogs love what they do, and the biggest reward they can have is to do it some more! Ricky, a springer spaniel, is a retrieve-aholic. So if he has done particularly well, I will set up a special retrieve for him to get, much to his joy! Physical contact is another good form of reward. Play with a favourite toy is a reward much used by trainers of assistance dogs and search and rescue dogs. Don't underestimate the importance of vocal praise as a reward – it's the form of positive reinforcement I use by far the most often, and it's the easiest and can be done instantly and from a distance. So if the dog is behaving well, say: 'Good boy, Ricky' (obviously not Ricky if he's not called Ricky) and use a lovely, warm soft tone of voice. Conversely, if he's behaving badly, say: 'Bad, Dutch, no,' very sharply in a really tough voice.

Being able to change your tone of voice is very important in dog training, and surprisingly it is one of the things people find most difficult to get right. Many men can't get their voice to go soft enough, and end up shouting at their dogs all the time. Some women find it a challenge to make their voices abrasive enough to catch a naughty dog's attention. The worst fault is to use the same tone of voice for both praise and reprimand, something I hear people doing all the time. If you don't *sound* cross, how will your dog know you *are* cross? It may not seem important, but elements like this are absolutely crucial to whether or not you will be successful in bringing up your pup to be perfect.

Understanding different types and breeds of dog

Different breeds and types of dogs are surprisingly different in their behaviour and attitude to training – and life in general. Even if you already have your pup, it's a good idea to know what to expect, and of course, if you are still deciding on a pup, getting to know the different breed groups will help you make a decision. For full descriptions of each breed and breed group, the website of the Kennel Club is internationally respected. Go to: www.thekennelclub.org.uk.

Hound group

This group includes beagle, basset, dachshund, whippet, Irish wolfhound, Scottish deerhound, borzoi, Afghan and greyhound as its best-known breeds. All of the hound group were originally used as hunting dogs. Even little dachshunds were originally used in Germany to hunt badgers – the German for badger is *dachs*. And at the other end of the scale, Scottish deerhounds were still used in the hunting of deer as late as the early twentieth century. Some hounds, like the foxhound, are closer to their roots than others. All hounds though, still have a

▶ *Ian and Wendy Openshaw's Irish wolfhound, Jess*

strong hunting drive. They are very easily distracted by smells and scent, whether the scent is blowing on the wind (air scent) or is coming from somewhere specific (ground scent). Of all the different types of dog they are among the most likely to chase animals and other dogs – often for very long distances. There are so many temptations in the countryside for hounds and you would be surprised what may have been in the local park a few hours before you have! Rabbits are a permanent problem for hound owners, but there are all sorts of other animals including foxes and even deer, that you may never have known lived nearby until you got a hound!

The smaller hounds like bassets and dachshunds are easier to manage, because they can't run so fast or so far, while for obvious

▼ *This dachshund is one of the hound group, and the breed was originally used to find badgers in Europe*

reasons long-legged hounds like deerhounds and Afghans can be quite a handful. Hounds are also one of the groups that has historically been encouraged to be noisy, or to 'speak', particularly when they are on a scent trail. They still have a tendency to 'give tongue' and can be very noisy if they are living in a group or within earshot of other dogs.

On the plus side they are beautiful and usually very healthy dogs. Historically they have always been kept in packs, so their pack imperative is still strong. This means they can be extremely loyal and highly bonded to their owner/trainer. A larger hound is probably not a good choice for a first-time dog owner, but beagles are very popular as family dogs.

Pastoral group

This is another group of working dogs, but originally they had the opposite job to hounds. While hounds were encouraged to hunt on behalf of humans, the pastoral dogs were kept to protect herds and flocks from wild predators like foxes, wolves and wild hunting dogs and indeed, the hunting dogs of human poachers. The group includes collies, sheepdogs, Australian cattle dogs, corgis, Pyrenean mountain dogs and Lancashire heelers. As well as protecting the flocks, the pastoral dogs were used to help manage the animals by herding them from place to place, rounding them up and separating them.

▲ *A French briard, Stormfield Amelie – the breed was originally used for shepherding in Europe*

▲ *A Rhodesian ridgeback, originally used for herding in southern Africa*

Like hounds, man has had pastoral, herding dogs from the time dogs were first domesticated. And like hounds, this group of dogs still retains the behaviours for which it was originally prized. It can be fiercely protective. It is also likely to chase other animals, in an instinctive need to herd them. Having always worked side by side with man, this group of dogs finds it easy to bond with their owner/trainer. Many experts consider the pastoral group to be the most intelligent of all the dog groups.

These characteristics have both pluses and minuses for us as owners. On the positive side, these breeds are tremendously trainable and extremely rewarding to work with. They perform at the highest level in competitions like obedience, agility and flyball. They are highly prized in modern working situations, especially in search and rescue, and of course, they continue to do the farm work they have done for thousands of years. However, there are drawbacks, especially for an inexperienced dog owner. They can become overprotective, as anyone will know who has ever tried to approach a farmer's kitchen door guarded by growling collies! They must be watched very carefully when they are around livestock and on farmland. They definitely have officer aspirations and can get a bit snappy and bossy unless you are assertive. As a highly intelligent dog, it is very important for them to be properly stimulated and trained – another reason why you will see so many herding dogs like collies do well in competitions.

Terrier group

The original all-round, multi-purpose working dog, there are now so many breeds of terrier that the Kennel Club has given them their own special category. Terrier owners would say that this is because terriers are a special dog that defies categorisation! The breeds include the largest,

▲ *Fidget, the Jack Russell terrier, showing how hardy the breed is*

the Airedale, which is about the size of a Labrador. There is also the famous Staffordshire bull terrier, which is short-legged but immensely strong and courageous. Other breeds include the Bedlington, fox, Norfolk, and Border terriers. Terriers were used for everything from vermin control, especially ratting, to bull-baiting and fighting. A terrier speciality which is still used today is their ability to go underground to seek out vermin. Many terrier breeds are short-legged, wiry-coated, tough and disproportionately courageous for their size.

As with all the working breeds, the group's original activities still influence their behaviour in good and bad ways. The courage, independence, toughness and good health of terriers make them among the most popular breeds worldwide, especially with country dwellers. Their generally small size makes them easy to take around and keep in the home. In rural situations, where people have lots of working dogs of different breeds doing different jobs, you will often find that it is only the terrier that gets to live in the house.

However, that independence and toughness does tend to make terriers rather hard to train. They are intelligent and make their own decisions – something they need to be able to do if stuck down a rabbit hole, but not necessarily helpful for their first-time dog trainers. Yet I have known dozens of teenage lads on the farms round me who permanently carry their terrier stuck down their shirt front, and the bond between the two is plain to see. Even if a terrier is going to be your first dog, you stand every chance of building a wonderful relationship if you are prepared to put in a few hard hours. Above all you need to have the right personality to lead – terriers definitely need an officer in charge!

Gundog group

The reason man domesticated dogs in the first place was for them to work on their behalf, so it's not surprising that out of the seven main groups of dog, there are almost no breeds that can't be traced back to a specific role. As the name suggests, the gundog group traces its origins to the hunting of animals with a gun. This is comparatively recent as opposed to hounds, which were used long before the invention of guns, and a huge percentage of gundog breeds are still used for their original purpose worldwide. The most famous of all the gundogs is the universally recognisable Labrador retriever, the most popular dog in America and Britain. Yet the good old Lab is in fact a rather a new breed, dating from only around 200 years ago. Other gundogs, including pointers and setters and spaniels, are also fairly new on the scene.

▶ *A fox-red Labrador retriever, now popular because of their unusual colour*

◀ *The traditional black Labrador retriever, the most popular breed in both UK and USA*

Compared with hunting or pastoral dogs, gundogs are the result of recent deliberate breeding strategies rather than accidental domestication thousands of years ago.

The group does have a strong drive to follow scent (in order to find game or recover wounded game) and to search for scent, but this is paired with a very marked desire to bond with humans and also great trainability. This may be because the gundogs as we know them never really existed in the wild, with their genetic blend having been created by man long after domestication. There is a reason why gundogs are the most popular breeds of all worldwide. They are generally very reliable and bond rapidly with their owners. The pointers and setters have a tendency to behave a little more like the hound group to which they are distantly related, but retrievers and spaniels were purpose built to dote on man, and they do.

Like the pastoral dogs, they are intelligent, and can go haywire unless given a sense of direction. Although they are easy to train, it is also important to train them, otherwise they will get bored and find trouble. As with all the working groups, they need to be watched when around livestock, but are generally very controllable.

Working group

This is something of a mixed group which the Kennel Club seems to have created to round up all the other originally working dogs that are not hounds, herders, terriers or gundogs. It includes St Bernard, Bernese Mountain, Dobermann, Rottweiler, mastiff, husky, Great Dane, and boxer. With such a mixed group it is hard to pick out overall characteristics, but breeds in this group do tend to be rather large. Originally they were used for all-round farm work including guarding, rescuing, herding, pulling a dog-cart (or sled in the case of the husky), and tracking. To this day many of them continue this work. Huskies are active in sled-racing, and you can still see St Bernards ready to go to work searching and rescuing if you happen to be skiing in the Alps. However, a few breeds in this group have developed a controversial reputation over the years – with Dobermanns and Rottweilers, for example, involved in various reported attacks. Rottweilers have adverse publicity, but the breeders and trainers who compete with these dogs in tracking competitions or use them in search and rescue, have nothing but praise for them. With the correct training, commitment and leadership from you, all these breeds can make perfect dogs. However, if you have a young family or limited space, or you are lacking in confidence, they probably wouldn't be the best place to start.

Utility group

It is quite hard to work out how the Kennel Club arrived at this grouping of breeds which includes bulldogs, Dalmatians, schnauzers, spitz, shih tzu, Lhasa apso, and poodles. Dalmatians, for example, were originally a working dog used to run alongside carriages and protect them from highwaymen. This rather romantic use is still commemorated today by American fire departments which like to have a pet Dalmatian living at the fire station (or fire house), and also in the new fashion for carriage-and-dog competitions. By contrast the Lhasa apso is famously a 'temple dog'; while poodles originated as gundogs in Europe. So there is a bit of everything in this group. If you have a pup from this group, or are considering buying one, go to the breed website for your chosen breed, or the Kennel Club's 'Discover Dogs' campaign. This will give you a specific insight into how your dog may behave. For obvious reasons, Dalmatians need a great deal of exercise. Poodles are surprisingly intelligent and tough. Since a wonderfully charismatic poodle won the Crufts show competition in 2014, it is likely that poodles will become popular again, which they thoroughly deserve. People tend to think of poodles as ridiculous because of the bizarre grooming sometimes inflicted on them by their owners, but in fact they are great dogs. A poodle crossed with a spaniel is the dog of choice for many assistance dog charities, including Hearing Dogs for Deaf People. Their coats hardly shed at all, which makes them a good choice for an indoor dog, and those with allergies. Some of the strange shapes of shaving actually originate from their use as water retrieving dogs, when their coats had to be shaved off to prevent them becoming waterlogged, but key areas like ankles, tail-ends and the loins were left for protection.

Toy group

This group comprises the miniature dogs which some refer to as 'handbag dogs' including bichon frisé, Pekingese, Cavalier King Charles, Maltese, papillon, Chihuahua, Yorkie, Pomeranian, and pug. It's unfortunate that the Kennel Club calls this group 'toy' as they are very much not toys. They may be small, but there's nothing little about their personalities, and they are often highly intelligent. In the course of writing about dogs I have met lots of Malteses, Chihuahuas, Yorkies, and of course the redoubtable pugs, and I have found them every bit as interesting as my own gundogs.

Miniature breeds and their owners tend to form very close bonds. Animal psychologists will tell you that this is as a result of the dogs' specific breeding to emphasise their baby-like attributes – large eyes, snub nose, small size, etc. Also, because of their small size, it is much easier to have a lot of very close contact with these dogs. An alternative name for the group is 'lap dog' and it's hard to imagine having a Rottweiler or a Great Dane as a lap dog! Because they fit in anywhere and don't take up a lot of space, the dogs are quite 'portable' so we do have a tendency to take them with us wherever we might be going, rather than leaving them at home as you might do a larger dog.

▲ *Spartacus, a pedigree pug – though classed as a 'toy' breed they deserve respect!*

Many of the assistance dog charities favour these smaller breeds, especially for hearing or medical alert work. They can live in a small apartment where the traditional Labrador retriever guide dog can't fit.

These charismatic little dogs deserve our respect – there's a lot more to them than just their size. They are generally very trainable and enjoy participating in all sorts of human events. For first-timers and where space is limited, the toy group is definitely worth thinking about. If you are thinking about competing and working with your dog, this will be hard for a toy breed. You see very few in competition (apart from showing) and search and rescue work would not be a forte! But if you are looking for a party companion, the pug's your dog.

Mongrels and crossbreeds

These are not recognised by the Kennel Club for showing or competition, but they are included in the *Companion Dog* category. Mongrels are the traditional 'Heinz 57' dog of unknown, and sometimes unguessable origin; but crossbreeds – a deliberate mating of two different breeds – are becoming very popular. Labradoodles (Labrador x poodle); spoodle (spaniel x poodle); and springadors (springer x Labrador) are all becoming increasingly fashionable. The main breeds being crossed are Labrador, spaniel, poodle and terrier.

Among the advantages are that the resulting cross tends to be very healthy – a phenomenon known as hybrid vigour. It is also thought that the cross will capture all the plus points and none of the minuses of the two breeds involved. For example, you could have the temperament of the Labrador without its tendency to develop hip problems. It doesn't always work this way, but many crossbreed owners are really enjoying their dogs.

The drawback is that, since the Kennel Club doesn't recognise crossbreed dogs, the breeding is unregulated. So if you do decide to have a crossbreed, or you have already bought one, be very careful to find out as much as you can about the puppy's background and about his breeder.

But perhaps the most successful dogs of all over the years have been those happy accidents that are a bit terrier, a bit whippet, a bit retriever, and a bit of fun. The traditional mongrel is often a pup full of joy, who turns out to be trainable and tough and likeable. You won't be able to take part in a lot of fancy, highly organised activities with him, but as a family all-rounder, many mongrels are every bit as good as a pedigree pup.

▲ *A crossbreed, with a touch of terrier, demonstrates 'hybrid vigour'!*

Try this questionnaire to discover your strengths and weaknesses as a dog owner.

THE PLUS POINTS

- Have you had a dog before? ☐
- Do you like the outdoors and walking? ☐
- Do you get on well with the people who work for you? ☐
- Are you fairly even-tempered? ☐
- Do you definitely want a dog? ☐
- Is your daily routine fairly predictable? ☐

The more boxes you tick in this section, the easier you are going to find it to enjoy owning and training your dog. If you can honestly tick all six boxes, the whole experience is likely to be great for you and the dog. You have already had a bit of experience and you will enjoy all the extra exercise you get from having a dog. You obviously don't have a problem showing your dog the leadership he needs, and can be relied on not to lose your temper or be impatient if things go a bit wrong. You have the right lifestyle to fit round a dog – and best of all, you really want a dog!

THE DEAL-BREAKERS

- Are you scared of animals? ☐
- Do you ever get violent? ☐
- Do you have addiction issues? ☐

THE BITS TO WORK ON

- Do you panic easily? ☐
- Do you lack confidence in various areas of your life? ☐

- Are you getting a dog just to keep the family happy? ☐
- Do you have rather a chaotic lifestyle? ☐
- Can you take criticism? ☐

Some of the issues flagged up by ticking these boxes mean that you may go on a bit of a journey when bringing up your puppy. However, they definitely won't prevent you from becoming a great dog owner and trainer. If you panic easily and lack confidence, your young dog will definitely challenge you from time to time. But every problem you overcome will have a positive effect in all areas of your life, not just the dog training. Many people report that owning and training a dog has given them the confidence to deal with all sorts of other issues, as well as improved their social life. If you are getting a dog just to keep the family happy, do make sure the family jolly well pulls its weight – they wanted the animal, so they must join in with looking after him. Chaotic lifestyles don't always fit in well with dogs, who prefer routine. If you love your wild lifestyle, the dog will adapt as long as you look after his welfare. On the other hand, if you are looking for a reason to settle down a bit, feeding the dog is always an acceptable excuse for leaving a party early! Those who find it hard to take criticism will sometimes find it hard to accept the self-discipline needed for successful dog training – and sometimes it is actually the dog who is taking the mickey! But it is worth plugging on for the sense of achievement when other people praise your dog.

These questions may seem obvious. Surely you don't buy a dog if you are scared of animals? But you would be surprised at the number of people I meet who are timid about and sometimes downright scared by very small puppies that they have bought. The tiniest nip or mini-growl has them rushing to the phone. If you have close friends or family, or a professional dog trainer, to help you overcome this, and you genuinely want to conquer your fears and are prepared to listen to advice, then the whole process can be tremendously uplifting. But even now, I often find myself asking why people have a puppy or a young dog when they so obviously don't like him or are afraid of him. If that's honestly the case, then you should probably consider a hamster. If you have serious issues, there can be a place for a dog in your life, and it can have a very positive impact. But the time is probably not yet. It is likely that a young and vulnerable puppy would not be a suitable companion.

Your Questions Answered about dog ownership

Q. Why do I need to train the puppy?

A. Although it's not a legal obligation, the reasons for training your puppy are similar to why you send your child to school. You want them to get the best out of life; to be able to participate in social events; to be good mannered and nice to be with. A little bit of training will mean your dog can go anywhere with you and not be a nuisance. He can enjoy socialising with other dogs. If he's obedient and well mannered life will be less stressful, for both you and him. Remember, a dog that doesn't come back when you call is a dog that has to stay on the lead.

Q. Will I have to look after the dog every day?

A. You or someone responsible will have to look after the dog every day for the rest of his life. The dog needs as a bare minimum feeding, watering, toileting and exercising every day. You cannot leave a dog to 'look after itself' even if you have provided some food and water. Nor should you leave a dog on his own for any long period of time, either in the house or outside. If you are going on holiday or for a big day out, make arrangements for the dog. If neighbours or family and friends aren't willing, there are plenty of professional dog walkers and dog sitters who advertise online or in the local papers. Ideally, of course, the dog should be so much a part of your life that the question of looking after him doesn't arise.

Q. Why does it matter if the dog is well behaved?

A. Well, your dog doesn't have to be a saint 24/7! Lots of the best dogs are quite naughty from time to time. Dear old Dutch was always being naughty, and at least it gave me plenty to write about. But it did also give me some very stressful times and sleepless nights. A dog that is badly behaved all the time isn't the companion to you and the family that he should be. And if you are not careful his bad behaviour can escalate into something more worrying. He may become aggressive towards your visitors, your children, even you. And having a dog that is polite means you can all have so much more fun. You can go to interesting places and have adventures together knowing he isn't going to let you down.

Q. I have been told a Labrador is the perfect breed – is that what I should get?

A. It certainly is what most people get! The Labrador retriever has been the most popular breed both in the UK and the USA for at least the last decade. This is because it is gentle, placid, loyal, friendly and easy to train. What's not to like? So why haven't I got one? They are quite large dogs. A full-grown Labrador is slightly too heavy for me to pick up easily. They do suffer from health problems, especially hip dysplasia (check out the breed website listed at the back of the book). Occasionally young male Labradors can become over-dominant if not properly trained. But these aren't the reasons why I don't have a Labrador. To be honest, I find them a bit boring. On the whole they are plodders, whereas the ride with my spaniels, if occasionally rocky, is always fun and exciting. When choosing your breed of dog, take your own personality into account. If the main thing is that you don't want anything too difficult, then the Lab's your lad!

Q. My puppy takes no notice of me at all. Why?

A. From reading this chapter, you can probably already guess at some of the reasons. First of all, do check your pup has no health problems. Very occasionally pups may be deaf or have poor eyesight or even brain developmental issues which can affect their ability to bond and learn. If the vet okays him, and he's OK with other people, then you have to look to yourself for the answer. Here are some questions you need to ask yourself:

Do I take enough notice of the puppy? If you ignore the puppy while you are at work all week and let the family look after him from day to day, you can't expect him to be all over you when you do occasionally turn up. I see this a lot with shooting dogs owned by businessmen. During the week the wife and children look after and train the dog. Then at the weekend the businessman comes home from work and wants to go shooting, and is furious that the dog treats him like a stranger – he is a stranger!

Am I charismatic enough with the puppy? In other words, are you someone interesting enough for him to want to know? Do you play with him, talk to him, have fun with him? Or do you just feed, water, toilet? Your puppy should think you are the best and most exciting thing since bones were invented.

Do I show leadership to the puppy? Do you insist that the puppy takes notice of you? If you constantly let him have his own way, he will soon get in the habit of just doing his own thing. That's bad news for the pup as well as for you, because it means he will miss out on a lot of dog–human things later in life. So do as an officer does and get in his face a little bit and make sure he knows the two of you are in this together.

HOW TO BE A PERFECT PUPPY OWNER

As you prepare to continue the upbringing of your puppy, this has been the time to think about the background skills it takes to own and train a dog. Here's a quick reminder of the things covered in this section.

The Canine Contract gave you a framework for asking not just what your dog can do for you, but what you can do for your dog.

Training the family and establishing routines are important to avoid stressful moments.

Thinking like a dog can enable you to communicate with him better, and anticipate what he is going to do next.

Leadership is a vital skill if you want to train your dog to the highest level and have him really bonded to you. Teaming this with understanding how to **positively reinforce** your dog's good behaviour will make training easy.

Check out the various **types of dog** to understand more about your puppy.

Now that you have a good understanding of the thinking behind what we do when living with our dogs, you can put it into practice as you start to train your dog. Part Three takes you and the pup through his first lessons starting aged three months old up to about six months.

PUPPY FROM THREE MONTHS TO ABOUT SIX MONTHS

Now that puppy is settled in and you have all established a good routine, it's time to move forward into the early stages of training. By now your puppy is house-trained; has completed his vaccinations and worming; and feels confident about you. This means that he's in exactly the right position to go out and start learning. This section of the book will take you through his early obedience and socialising work. You will teach the basic vocabulary and start using verbal instructions as well as introducing a whistle and the lead. And you will learn much more about understanding your pup and his personality to help him achieve his full potential.

▶ *A strong pup makes nothing of carrying this cricket ball, although a tennis ball is more usual*

Puppy personality profiling

Just like humans, dogs have different personality traits. They can be shy or timid or bouncy or bold. Sometimes clever dogs can be manipulative just like people. And there are lots of dim but adorable dogs who don't have a lot going on in their brains, but make up for it by showing plenty of bonding with their owner. And again, like humans, dogs with different personalities and levels of intelligence react differently to teaching. We all know five- and six-year-old girls who are button-bright and learn everything quickly and easily the moment they start school. Or there are the shy ones who may take a little longer, but often turn out to be very academic as they grow up. And then there are the goofy teenagers who go through a phase of finding everything just impossible to get right! All these different types learn in different ways, but if we understand their learning needs and adapt to them, everybody gets there in the end.

It's the same with puppies. The top professional dog trainers spend a lot of time working out the personality traits of each new young dog they start to train. Based on what they understand about the pup, they will often use very different techniques from one pup to another. As first-time dog owners, of course we aren't in a position to do that. And many people who are inexperienced with dogs find it quite difficult to work out what kind of personality their puppy has – and what his agenda might be.

The foundation bitch of my 'Gournaycourt' breeding line was a highly intelligent little black cocker spaniel with white tips to her paws, whom we all called Tippy. Slightly unusually, she was already a few months old when I got her from a friend, so I didn't know her as a little puppy. She went on to become very successful in competition, but all her life she would belly-crawl and worm and go over on her back in an ultra-submissive way when you asked her to do something she didn't want to do, such as jump in the car or go on her bed.

She did it from the first night I got her home, and I can remember thinking, 'oh, this is the last thing I need, yet another animal, and this one's a wimp.' Yet she wasn't a coward at all. In competition she was both highly intelligent and almost insanely brave. Then I'd ask her to jump back into the vehicle, and there she was belly-crawling and shivering as if to say '… oh, don't beat me, please.' I was trying and trying to get to the bottom of this issue, and in exasperation I said to her: 'Look, Tippy, I know every single person who's ever touched you and no one has ever, ever done or said an unkind thing to you, so what is this all about?' And then I realised, she was what human psychologists call 'passive aggressive'. She got her way by *pretending* to be very submissive and by subtly implying that we were all terribly cruel to her. She would guilt us all out so much that inevitably we would pick her up and give her a little cuddle before gently lifting her into her travelling pen. So instead of being told off for being naughty and disobeying an instruction to go in the pen, she was being rewarded! There was in fact nothing at all submissive about Tippy, despite her body language; she had us all wrapped round her paw.

So it's very important as you start training your puppy to understand what a complex little character he may turn out to be, and adapt your training style accordingly. But as you can tell from Tippy, it's not always easy to work out your pup, so I have devised a unique **Puppy Personality Profiler** to help you understand your pup. It includes methods and questions to assess your pup's basic intelligence, his athletic ability, and his attitude to life. Over a couple of weeks you can do a few of the exercises. Don't do them all on the same day or you and the puppy will be exhausted! Remember too, that though very simple, these are quite demanding little tasks for a young pup. There is no 'pass' or 'fail', but put the three strands together and you will have a good idea of your pup's overall personality and potential in his future training.

◀ *Start to gain insight into your puppy's personality*

INTELLIGENCE TESTS

Note: These games are only for testing your pup's intelligence, and not for training. Don't repeat the test or use it as a training exercise.

1. *Treat or Trick?*

Get a little edible treat out for the pup – something he likes, whether it might be a dog choc drop or a piece of sausage or a bit of cheese. Show it to pup so he knows you have it. Then take a cup or bowl. Put it upside down on the floor and put the treat underneath. What does your pup do?

A. Makes a bee-line for the bowl and manages to get it turned over and get the treat out.

B. Sniffs around a bit but can't quite get the bowl tipped back and eventually gives up.

C. Is basically completely flummoxed by the whole disappearing treat problem!

2. *Hide'n'Seek*

Take the pup playing in the garden or round the house, or anywhere safe for pup to be running free that has hiding spots for you. Pick a moment when his attention isn't fully on you or create a diversion by throwing his favourite toy, and then hide where you can't quite be seen, but you can secretly watch him. What does he do?

A. Grabs his toy and instantly comes running up to you in your hiding spot.

B. Notices you are gone and starts looking round for you, eventually tracking you down.

C. Doesn't immediately notice you are gone, and loses concentration generally.

3. Spot the Ball

Using pup's favourite toy or tennis ball, start playing with him round the garden or house. Next you need to hide a couple of toys without pup seeing. You can either put him in his pen for a moment while you go and hide the toys or you can get someone else to distract him by cuddling him or even covering his eyes. The truest test though, is if pup is in his pen and not anywhere around when you are doing the hiding. Don't overdo the number of things you hide, two is plenty. Now get pup and bring him into the area where the toys/tennis balls are hidden. Don't give him any instructions or play with him. Just let him potter around doing his own thing while you watch. What does he do?

A. Finds his first toy instantly and brings it over to you. When you then take it and let him play around again, he also finds the next toy and again brings it over to you.

B. Finds his first toy quite quickly and comes over to you to play, but when you take the toy, he wants to continue to play with you and the toy, without bothering to look for any more toys.

C. Stays with you, playing round your feet and doesn't really bother to go off searching for toys, although he may come across one accidentally.

4. What's in a Name?

Be careful with this test, as it can have a confusing effect on the pup. It is useful though, as a way of finding out how pup is really reacting to you – whether he genuinely knows his name and responds to it, or whether he is just rather overdependent on you and will come over to you anyway. So let the pup play around and get quite a little distance from you. If you are indoors it should be the other side of the room but not a different room. If you are outdoors, the opposite edge of a normal sized lawn is a good distance. Now call the pup, but use a completely different sounding name. So if his name is 'Bramble', call 'Coal'. Don't use any of the body language you would normally use for calling pup, like kneeling down or clapping your hands or patting your thighs. Just call, what does he do?

A. Stops what he is doing to look at you, but doesn't come, and perhaps puts his head on one side.

B. Continues playing and takes no notice of you.

C. Comes rushing up goofily to you.

WHAT THE ANSWERS TELL YOU

Straight As:

Although they are just modified play behaviour, these little tests are actually quite challenging for a young pup. If your puppy sails through them, then you obviously have a youngster that is naturally highly intelligent. In addition to this he is also displaying a linked characteristic which dog handling professionals call 'work motivation' or 'drive'. This basically means that not only is the puppy bright enough to learn and achieve a lot, but he also wants to do it and gets a lot of canine fulfilment out of it. These are the kind of pups that very often grow up to be working dogs, perhaps in emergency services or as assistance dogs, or to compete in all sorts of areas. They are quite rare to come across, and usually crop up in the recognised working breeds like border collies, German shepherds, Labrador retrievers and spaniels. These pups soak up basic training like a sponge – BUT! – for first-time dog owners it can be a bit of a challenge to keep up with them and keep everything going in the right direction. To have the best results and enjoyment with this type of pup, it is a good idea to get some experienced help. There is lots of information in Part Five, and at the back of the book, about training schemes and clubs you can join. You don't want your super-bright pup becoming delinquent because you have run out of stuff for him to do!

Middling, mainly Bs:

The vast majority of our family companion dogs will slot happily into this category, scoring an A on the occasional favourite exercise and dropping to a C on something confusing, but mostly firmly hitting the B grade for achievement. The good news is that this is an ideal level of intelligence for your first dog! Really, if you don't have a lot of experience and are just looking for a fun four-pawed friend for all the family, then being responsible for bringing up the next Lassie is really rather more than you had signed up for. I often wonder how Superman's foster parents felt when they began to realise what their boy could do! But a middling B-grader dog is no problem for anyone. Often the B-graders are very nearly as intelligent as the straight A pups but lack that additional quality of high motivation and drive. Your pup is certainly bright enough to learn everything you want to teach him without much difficulty, and you will have the fun of learning together.

Contentedly C grades:

I'm afraid there's no way of sugar-coating this. If he rarely rises to the dizzy heights of a B grade, then we have to face it that your dog is dim! On the plus side, at least you have discovered this now, rather than at the end of months or even years of frustration and failed training attempts. I didn't realise that Dutch's IQ was on a par with a well-made house brick until I'd been entering competitions for at least a year, assuming that just because the rest of his family were officer class, he would be too. With a good idea of what your pup's potential is, you can adjust your expectations and training methods to fit. Nor is there anything wrong at all with a dim dog. They are usually the most affectionate and loyal of all; just don't expect him to be bringing you the calculations for filling in your tax return. The drawback is that intellectually challenged dogs are harder to train, and unlikely, ultimately, to achieve all the things you may be hoping for. When training, you may find he has a short attention span and poor memory. He might appear to learn something quite quickly, but forget the lesson again almost immediately. Or he may find the simplest things, like learning his name, ridiculously difficult. You will just have to be patient and adjust your expectations. Take comfort that if you make any mistakes, it's unlikely to do much damage!

ATHLETIC ABILITY

Note: These challenges are only for testing your pup's basic athletic ability, and not for training. Don't repeat the challenges or use as training exercises.

1. *Chase me Charlie*

Get your pup's attention and set off at a bit of a jog – preferably in the garden. Remember your pup is still only very young so it's just for a few moments and not very fast, but it will still give a very good impression about his co-ordination and developing physical abilities. Lots of puppies will fall over their paws a bit. I remember a litter of mine that when tiny used get around more by rolling than running but they all did very well as they grew up. Some pups will be up with you very quickly, which is a great sign. Do watch carefully though, for any signs that pup's front and hind legs are out of co-ordination and he seems to be running faster in front than behind (or vice versa) or if he is actually reluctant to run.

2. *Bending Race*

This little game is a wonderful way of checking pup's paw-to-eye co-ordination. Get three flower pots and place in a line, far enough apart for you to weave in and out of them. If you like you can stick a bamboo cane in each one to make weaving poles. Now start walking in and out of the pots, hopefully with your pup following you. If you can get to the stage where he has learnt to weave in and out on his own, definitely consider agility training when he is older.

3. *Jumping*

Lots of working-breed dogs are excellent jumpers, as the skill is frequently needed. Build a small, safe obstacle. If you are indoors, a couple of cushions or a rolled-up blanket are ideal. Outdoors, be careful that any obstacle you use doesn't have anything sticking out or sharp bits that could injure the pup. Make sure that the take-off and landing sides are safe and not hard or slippery. A small log or a puddle makes a good obstacle. Jump over it yourself and encourage pup to follow you over. Lots of athletic, confident pups will have a go at getting over all on their own without any encouragement from you. In fact with this kind of pup, much of your time will be spent hauling them out of streams or lifting them down from walls. You will learn a lot about your pup's general character from this exercise, as well as his physical talent.

4. *Strong Dog*

Carrying objects comes naturally to dogs, and it is something humans encourage them to do, both for work and for recreation and competition. If you think you might be interested in doing formal retrieving work with your dog later, you can check out his aptitude now. He is certainly likely to be carrying little toys and tennis balls round. But try him with something a bit more awkward or slightly heavier. Pet shops stock a number of different retrieving objects, and you can also buy canvas carrying dummies from specialist gundog training suppliers (more details at the back of the book). See how your puppy reacts to finding one of these in his play space. The top pups will find a way to pick it up or drag it, no matter how difficult. A puppy who is less highly motivated or not so strong will probably give up after a few attempts or even ignore the object.

◀ *Test a strong pup with heavier items*

The following are six different attitude and personality types you can often see in pups. I have called them after well-known fictional characters. Your pup is very likely to fit into one or the other. By watching him closely over a few days to observe how he reacts to different situations, you will be able to spot his character type.

1. *Just William*

Most people's favourite personality of dog, this pup doesn't have an ounce of malice in him and is always trying to do the right thing, but somehow he keeps on getting into scrapes and trouble. This is the pup who climbs out of the playpen; who manages to get the kitchen cupboard open; who tries to jump a stream and doesn't make it. This kind of pup is intelligent, athletic, affectionate and highly trainable, but he does need to be trained. Without a little bit of sensible, serious training, those little scrapes that were so amusing at six months old become definite problems as the pup grows up. Make sure your 'Just William' knows boundaries, and be firm over the difference between right and wrong. Just Williams are so charming and amusing in their antics that they often get away with too much. In fiction Just William

▶ *A 'Just William' type pup*

(William Brown) was the leader of a gang of children who called themselves The Outlaws – don't let your pup grow up to be a real outlaw.

2. *Lassie*

This character needs no introduction – the archetypal hero dog. Interestingly you can spot 'Lassie' types really early on. Even in the litter, they display natural leadership among their brothers and sisters, not just by being the boss but also in looking out for them. Lassie pups score straight As in intelligence and athleticism tests, exactly as Just William pups may do. The difference is in how they use their talent. A Lassie is instinctively more responsible in his behaviour and doesn't seem to get into scrapes. Your Lassie pup learns just as quickly how to

◀ *Fizz mastered all her little tests from a very young age*

get out of the playpen, but chooses to remain in it because you asked him to. Lassies will bring you anything they find and offer it to you for checking. When you are out on walks and playing together, Lassie will constantly keep an eye on you and will check-in with you from time to time without being asked. Lassies not only learn quickly, but they don't forget things, nor do they get bored, and they have excellent concentration. I have been lucky enough to train a couple of Lassies over the years and it is a privilege. However it is also a huge responsibility! I am constantly worrying about not meeting their high standards, or not giving them the opportunity to fulfil their huge potential. This may sound ridiculous now – he's just a puppy after all – but if you are ever fortunate enough to have one, you will recognise the pressure. There's a definite case for saying: 'Lassie? Get help!'

3. *Winnie-the-Pooh*

Poor old Pooh is a pup of little brain, but very good-hearted. Like Pooh, these pups often grow up to have a bit of a weight problem as they get older, and will eat anything, including not just condensed milk, but the tin it comes in. Labrador retrievers are notorious for having Pooh tendencies. You can spot a Pooh pup very early on. They relax easily and are laid-back in their attitude. They never lose their appetites and are terrible food thieves, regularly breaking into fridges and stealing from the dining table. They are loyal, affectionate and keen to please, but can be rather lazy. Because of their ability not to worry about things, they find basic training very easy but sometimes they don't have the brain power to go a lot further. If you can get on top of his appetite, a Pooh pup makes a great family or first-timer's dog. It is important not to let your Pooh get too overweight as it will affect his health over the years. So make sure food is locked away properly and don't be tempted to give way to his constant begging for treats.

4. *The Artful Dodger*

The big difference between this type of pup and the Just William pup is socialisation and bonding. Just William and The Artful Dodger both do crimes! But Just William didn't mean to, and is usually caught and told off. The Artful Dodger is rarely caught out, and doesn't attempt to mend his ways. Professional dog trainers used to call this type of dog 'hard', and some breeds were notorious for throwing up a lot of hard dogs. These were then trained through a punishment system, which was almost always a failure, particularly when attempted by inexperienced trainers. With these tough pups, their attitude is that the punishment is worth the fun of the crime. With this pup, once he has first nipped your ankle or nicked the TV remote control, he will do it again and again, seemingly unaffected by any steps you may take. This is generally not a good type of young dog for inexperienced people or young families to take on.

However, there are many ways round The Artful Dodger, as long as you spot him in time. In his testing The Artful Dodger presents a confusing picture – scoring very highly on some of his intelligence, yet apparently not knowing his name. He will be generally very inconsistent in his behaviour. Unlike other types of dog, he will tend to repeat something even though you have told him off for it. There will be special advice on this as we go through the training, and one of the important things to remember is not to get into a nuclear arms race of punishment. In the early stages, predicting and avoiding situations is the priority.

5. Piglet

Dear little Piglet is an easy pup-type to spot. He was the shy one in the litter, and he dithers in the doorway to his pen. He's not a confident pup at all and loud noises or sudden movements bother him. He doesn't appear to be very inquisitive – unlike most puppies – and this is usually because he is too scared to investigate or get into scrapes. So this pup is certainly no Artful Dodger or even a Just William, and there is a tendency to assume that he will therefore be easy to train and ideal for novices and families. In fact many experienced trainers would far rather do battle with an Artful Dodger than try to cope with Piglet's neuroses! The main problem is that if Piglet is pressured too hard, he can become defensively aggressive. Where a bold, confident idiot of a young dog will come bouncing up and lick you all over, a Piglet will cower and then suddenly turn and snap at you. So spot your Piglet early on, keep the pressure off, and let him get a lot of success in his training to build up his confidence – there will be advice on this as we go through the training.

6. *Uriah Heep*

I've already described the manipulative behaviour of my Uriah Heep pup, Tippy. It is a personality type that crops up fairly often in working breeds, especially in the high achievers. These pups are very intelligent and learn quickly how to do things – but they want to do it their own way! However they don't want to be downright disobedient and get involved in a confrontation they probably won't win, so they devise methods of getting their way without you actually noticing they are doing it. As you can probably tell, the Uriah Heep is a personality type I adore! Once you have recognised their agenda, training is great fun, and in the end you can achieve so much, because the pup is very intelligent. One of the most rewarding aspects of training any animal is meeting one that is independent and capable, and building a true partnership together. That's what this book is all about – and a few months down the line you will be enjoying the same thing.

Start with obedience

Obedience is one of the cornerstones of your puppy's training. The very best kind of obedience to generate from your puppy is something that he doesn't have to think about. It is the kind of obedience that develops from the puppy instinctively feeling that you are in charge of him and his well-being. Sometimes people call this 'bonding'. People who are considering buying a partly trained dog rather than a puppy often ask me: 'Oh, but surely it will be too late for him to bond with me? I have to get a puppy to make sure we bond.'

Bonding is in fact a very imprecise term. Zoologists prefer to use the word 'imprint'. This is the instinct by which the young of any animal latches on to the adult (usually its mother) who will ensure its early survival. Imprinting is what causes a baby mammal to suckle and to form an attachment within its family group. This is loosely where the bond develops. Some animal trainers do use 'imprinting' quite deliberately when training wild rather than domesticated animals.

Falcon trainers will ensure they are there when an egg hatches so that the young bird of prey is imprinted on to them. This often happens, with variable results, with large mammals that have been rescued from a wild situation at birth, or that are born and raised in captivity.

You will be glad to know there is no need to go to these sorts of lengths when training your pup! You want him to grow up to be a well-adjusted young dog who knows perfectly well that he is a dog and you are a human, and also understands exactly what the boundaries of his behaviour are – because you have shown him. So there's no need for imprinting, and the type of 'bonding' you are looking for is one of mutual cooperation and respect. This stems from having a very clearly defined relationship in the first place. Puppy must grow up in a climate where he never thinks twice about the fact that you are the person who not only looks after him but also is in charge of him.

Boundaries

You must have clear boundaries for your pup – but in order to do that you need to know yourself what the boundaries are. Everybody has different boundaries for their dogs. In the countryside, people like myself with dogs that work outside all the time don't have them in the house very much. The dogs are big, bouncy, muddy, messy and don't really settle and relax for their downtime while they are still with humans. So my dogs have their own 'dogs' room' and the boundary is that they don't come in the house. More people set a boundary that the dog can come in the kitchen and utility areas, but not the posh bits like the sitting room. Some people have their dogs not just in the sitting room but sitting up alongside them on the sofa, or they let their dogs sleep in bed with them. Personally I'm not a big fan of this. Letting the dog get literally on top of you usually gives him the idea that he is on top of you in all ways.

Boundaries don't just apply physically to where your dog goes, but also what he does. Again, working dogs are taught very firm boundaries because they will need them in their work. For example, my dogs aren't allowed to chase, because when they are working in competitions or in the countryside where there are lots of birds and animals, chasing can be damaging for the wildlife. Companion dogs can be a lot more unstructured in their play and so chasing is allowed, but certainly not catching a squirrel or nipping a human being. But some people even allow their little dogs to nip or snap and think it's very funny. If these dogs happen to be the same dogs who are also allowed to sit up on the arm of the sofa at the height of a human head, a nip on the ankle all too easily becomes a bite on the nose. So you can see how important boundaries are.

▶ *Set your boundaries where you would like them to be*

You need to decide now what your boundaries will be for the puppy, and stick to them. Here's a boundary setting chart. Just work your way through the answers to give yourself a clear picture of how you want things to be:

In house or out of house? ....

In just kitchen and utility or the whole of downstairs?...................

Allowed upstairs too?...

Allowed in bedroom? Even in bed?.......................................

Some playing and chasing under supervision?...........................

Unlimited free playing?..

Chasing after everything?..

Chewing shoe laces?...

A little bit of hand-mouthing, play tugging?...........................

Nipping the ankles?..

Doing his own thing?..

Being fed treats from the family dinner?.................................

Really only you and your family can answer these questions; different boundaries work for different situations and different dogs. Working and competition dogs like mine have very different boundaries from pet dogs, and these may sometimes appear harsh and strict. Farm dogs spend nearly all their time in the farmyard and often live permanently in the back of a truck. There are some fantastic husky sled dogs who live up in the Cairngorms and their homes are old whisky barrels, even in two feet of snow. My own dogs don't get away with much when it comes to being disobedient. Yet all these different dogs are living fantastic lives doing doggy things and having experiences and adventures that they certainly wouldn't swap for an evening in front of the telly. But if your own life is spent mainly in front of the telly,

▲ *It's your decision to allow pup up on the sofa, bed or other furniture*

then it makes sense for your dog to be sharing that with you. So feel free to set your boundaries according to your own needs and lifestyle – but once set, puppy must abide by them!

Right and wrong; yes and no

Now that you have decided on your boundaries, obviously puppy needs to know what those boundaries are. Many trainers rely on what could be called the 'enforcement method' to do this. Basically, you let the puppy find the boundary by breaking it, and give him a little telling off and he won't do it again. The late Keith Erlandson, who was one of the most successful gundog trainers of all time, told me that he felt this was both illogical and unfair. If the pup didn't know in the first place that this was a wrong thing to do, then punishing him is unjust. Suppose they reduce the speed limit in your town centre to 20mph, as many are doing, but they don't bother to put new signs up? So the first you know about it is when you are getting three points for speeding – you'd be finding a lawyer pretty quickly!

Keith's view was that you create a situation where it is clear to the puppy what is right and wrong, so that the chances of him getting into trouble by accident are very much reduced. For example, you may have a boundary that your pup is allowed into the downstairs of the house, but not upstairs. The 'enforcement method' would let the puppy try to scramble upstairs (which any pup worth his salt is going to try to do) but then tell him off. Instead simply putting a child-gate across the staircase shows the pup quite clearly that is somewhere he can't go, without any need for any incidents.

If your boundary is that your puppy is allowed to chew old outdoor shoes, but not to chew your smart work shoes, then it is very simply a matter of not allowing him in the room where you keep your good clothes. I have never understood people who whinge constantly about their pups and grown-up dogs chewing their stuff and their furniture. Human beings have opposable thumbs and even brains (in some cases): if you don't want it chewed, don't leave it where puppy can chew it!

So whenever you can, remember that prevention is better than cure with obedience to boundaries. If pup never gets the opportunity to do a bad thing, he will be much less likely to get involved in badness generally. This is particularly important if you think you may have an Artful Dodger pup. Because of their 'hardness', punishment as a discouragement from boundary-breaking is often ineffective. So with these dogs, keep them out of trouble right from the beginning. It's a good method to use with 'Piglets' as well, because being very secure in their knowledge of their boundaries makes them feel safer and more confident, and as a result, more relaxed.

Inevitably though, the time will come when puppy is learning by pushing at the boundaries. Work out which boundaries your puppy is likely to push and be prepared. Pooh-type puppies, for example, are motivated mainly by food. This leads to hilarious situations. Your Pooh has never attempted to get upstairs or open the door to the dining room, so you assume he's a very good boy and don't think twice about putting the roast on the dinner table and wandering out to get everybody, leaving the dining room door slightly ajar, returning moments later to find no roast at all, and a Pooh that suddenly seems to have discovered miraculous powers of door-opening and table-climbing. The answer is, of course, he never went in the dining room up until now because you didn't leave the roast in there before! Learn to understand your puppy's hot buttons.

Managing disobedience

First of all you need an understanding of what type of disobedience you are encountering. There are three main behaviours that come across as disobedience:

1. *Pushing boundaries*

Every pup is going to do this at some stage and it is very easy to deal with. You need to intervene instantly. The moment you see your puppy doing the wrong thing, go over to him and stop him from doing it. When puppies are small, the easiest way to do this is by picking them up. At the same time, say sharply and firmly, 'No!' You can also say 'Ach, ach' or 'Bad!' If you do this absolutely immediately, and always, every time the pup does something naughty, then you will never need to do anything more. You will also find you need to do it less and less often. But you must be consistent. You must always tell pup off when he has broken a boundary, not just when you happen to be in a bad mood. And you must always do it immediately, which is why it is advisable to supervise your puppy as much as possible when he is young.

2. *Failing to understand an instruction*

As your training of puppy continues, you will very soon be adding in instructions as well as boundaries to his life. As well as things he mustn't do, there will also be things he should do because you have asked him to do them. These are instructions like 'come' or 'sit'. It is quite important to recognise whether or not your puppy really understands what you want from him when you give him these instructions. Hints that he is confused include looking at you with his head on one side; or perhaps trying to do it but giving up; or looking not very confident; or rolling over on his back in a very submissive way. When you spot this you know he's not being naughty or disobedient; he just doesn't understand. So you need to make your instruction a lot clearer. The best way is to go back a step, like revision. So check back on Part One, where puppy first began to learn those very basic words, and start the routine again. Definitely don't punish a pup for not understanding you.

▲ *Learn your pup's body language, head on one side often means confusion*

3. *Deliberately disobeying instructions*

It's usually quite easy to tell if a pup is deliberately disobeying you. For example, he usually comes when you say his name and ask him to 'come', but today you have given him this instruction while he is playing with his favourite toy. He stops briefly and looks at you, and then continues to do whatever it is he is doing. This is very definitely the 'old two paws' and must not ever be tolerated! As we have discussed, it's not a question of punishment, but correction. He isn't allowed to get away with being disobedient, but is firmly reminded of what you expect him to do. In the case of 'come' you can walk over to him and gently grab him and drag him to you at the same time as removing his toy.

If you get this right now, while the pup is still so young, you won't have problems in the future. I can't stress this enough! Never, ever repeat an instruction to a dog if you are sure he has understood what you want. If there is one thing to learn from this book, this will absolutely transform the way our dogs behave. If you repeat the instruction once the dog has deliberately disobeyed it, he will continue to disobey it because there is no reason for him to do otherwise. If he does this often enough, the instruction you have so painstakingly taught him becomes completely meaningless. You have effectively deprived yourself of one of the powers that makes man different from animals – that of speech, of complex vocalisation. If you keep babbling meaningless sounds at your pup/young dog, he will lose all respect for you, and that is basically the end of training, and of a proper companionship.

This is so fundamental, and so obvious, but just go out into a dog exercise area tomorrow and have a listen. I am absolutely sure you will hear people calling: 'Come here, Bubbles, come, come, come on Bubbles, there's a good boy, come, come here,' for more or less as long as you can be bothered to listen. Don't be one of those people. Be one of the cool people who mutters 'Rufus, co..' or just chirrups a little whistle and the dog is at your feet before you've finished the word. It feels great when they do that, by the way!

Socialising

Getting your puppy used to being with people, with other dogs, with other animals, and in all sorts of different situations is important. There's a certain amount of socialisation that can be done in the house and garden before puppy has his full immunity, and that's discussed in Part One. But once the vet has given the all clear that pup is allowed into the outside world, it's time to start socialisation proper. The best place to start is a local open space, usually a dog-friendly park or

▲ *A trip to the seaside is a great socialising experience*

country walk. You can also start on puppy socialisation classes, usually organised by your vet. Check whether the places you want to take the pup are genuinely dog-friendly. High-street shopping is not a good idea as he won't be allowed in the shops. But I recently took a young golden cocker pup to our local outdoor Farmers' Market, which was a huge success, although it did take me twice as long as usual to get the shopping done.

Friends' homes work well as it is a nice, controllable environment. Anything you do outdoors works, but remember that pup is too young to come on long walks or to go jogging or cycling with you. The aim of socialisation is for the pup to learn by encountering lots of new experiences and managing to deal with them. So hearing cars and loud noises is good, as they can get used to how to react and watch how you react. They can also learn how to respond to strange dogs or people, with you reminding them of what you want them to do. Obviously you won't let them go rushing up and bounce all over them, so your pup will be beginning to get more obedience training while he is socialising.

You will also find out a lot more about your pup's personality from how he responds to different environments. Some puppies who appear very confident at home are rather shy when they go out in public. When I started socialising Ricky I took him to a local beauty spot where he met a lady coming towards him with a pushchair, and this quite large, bouncy springer spaniel suddenly turned into a quaking wreck, taking cover behind me and shivering. It was all rather embarrassing having to explain to the lady that my dog thought she was a dragon!

Depending on your lifestyle, socialising can sometimes feel a bit of an irritation. It is time-consuming and doesn't seem to be contributing anything concrete to training. Solo's early puppyhood came along at a very busy and stressful time in my life, and to be honest, I didn't devote as much time to socialising him as I normally would. He's grown up fine, but I do notice that loud noises bother him and he is a wimp about thunderstorms, unlike all my other dogs who love them and want to go and retrieve whatever it is that has fallen out of the sky with such a loud crash!

THE BASIC WORDS OF INSTRUCTION

At between three and six months old, your puppy isn't ready for 'big school' formal training yet, but he is already learning very rapidly, so it's a good time to start teaching him the basic vocabulary that you will be using in his training and throughout his life. The good news is that if all has been going well so far, your puppy should already know the important words.

The big four little words:

His name – your very first point of contact, and will remain the best communication throughout training. You will be teaching your dog automatically to hear his name and respond to it. At first he will come towards you when you call his name, but as his training progresses, his name will become a call sign which says: 'take notice, I'm about to give you an instruction.'

Come – means what it says on the tin, and always results in pup coming. As we have discovered in Part One, 'come' is initially taught by being linked with the pup's name and various encouragements from you through body language and play. As training progresses, 'come' will be a much more precise command and the pup will come to you when asked by whistle, hand gesture, or the original voice command.

Sit – taught with the feed bowl right from the beginning, your pup should already understand the word and fairly reliably obey it even when it is not connected with his feed bowl. As training progresses, 'sit' will pair with 'come' to be the two big cornerstones of all your pup's future work. You will teach your puppy to sit whenever he hears the verbal instruction, or when asked by whistle, or hand gesture. You will eventually get to the point where he will sit instantly and look at you, no matter where he is (as long as he is within earshot) or what he is doing. Learning to sit promptly and obediently could one day save your dog's life – if for example he is about to run into a dangerous place. If you want to do lots of interesting, adventurous things with your dog, it is going to be a really important part of his training.

No – not really an instruction, but a word that your pup needs to understand very thoroughly! Hopefully you won't have to say it very often, but when you do, that's it, end of. Dogs are very black and white in their outlook. 'Maybe' and 'perhaps another time' or the dreaded 'we'll see' might work with young children, but are just too complex for dogs. When the boss has spoken, and the word he or she has spoken is 'No', that's all there is to it.

The power of four:

No matter what your dog goes on to do in his grown-up life and training, whether he becomes a rocket scientist or a rambling companion, the big four little words are at the core of all his training. Obedience dogs, gundogs, sheepdogs – they are all being trained and handled using refinements of just those four words. And hey, your pup is more than halfway to knowing them! Between three and six months there is no need to teach any more verbal instructions. Instead concentrate on getting these absolutely spot on. Don't make a huge thing of it. Keep them as part of play and use play and toys as rewards. Don't overdo them either. They need to be a natural part of pup's life with you. So if you want him to come for a reason, or you need him to sit, ask him to – but don't constantly stop him in the middle of playing to make him sit. In Part Four we will be learning how to build the big four into serious training. We will teach pup to obey them at a distance, and to combine them into complex exercises, along with other subsidiary commands.

Starting the whistle

Most dog lovers associate a dog whistle with serious working dogs like sheepdogs, or with competitions. In fact whistles work brilliantly for all dog owners, and even if you never plan to do anything more with your dog than stroll round the park, there are many reasons for having a whistle. It is a very precise form of communication, and it is very personal to you and your dog. No two dog trainers/owners make exactly the same sound on their whistle. And of course, it is private between you and your dog. Only the two of you know exactly what a certain sound on the whistle means, so if you are blowing your whistle to get him to come back because he is being naughty, no one else need know about it. This would be rather useful with the human family! I often think training children to respond to the whistle might save a lot of grief …

▶ *Why not take the opportunity to train your child to the whistle as well as pup?!*

The dog whistle is usually attached to a lanyard and worn like a pendant round the neck, and as mentioned earlier, it is quite a useful 'badge of office' reminding you that you are responsible for the dog whenever you are wearing it, or whoever is wearing it. There is no need to get a fancy 'silent' whistle or a stag's horn or anything like that. For ordinary training the basic 'Acme' plastic whistle that gundog trainers often use is fine, and you don't have to be training a gundog to use one. Check out the back of the book for whistles and where to buy them. I have about half a dozen as I am always forgetting them, so I will have one hanging in the kitchen, in the dog's room, in the car, in my handbag, etc.

There are three basic whistle commands: 'come'; 'stop'; 'turn round'. In combination, these three commands mean that you can control exactly what your dog does and where he goes, even at a considerable distance. If you have ever watched sheepdog trialling competitions you will probably have marvelled at the extraordinary way the shepherds can move their collies so precisely for such a long distance away, but if you listen carefully, you will find they are using careful combinations of very simple commands that any of us can teach our dogs.

These are the whistle commands I use:

1. 'pip, pip, pip, pip, pip' repeatedly for about three to five pips means 'come'.

2. One long 'peeeeep' means 'stop' and I expect a fully trained dog not just to stop but to sit up and look at me to see what we are going to do next.

3. Just two gentle sounds – 'pip,pip' means turn round and go in the other direction. Many people never use this third command, but if you do get interested in various dog training activities it comes in useful.

The 'come' whistle

Even when your pup is less than six months old, you will do no harm by beginning to introduce the 'come' whistle. Leave the other whistle commands until his is older – these are discussed in detail in Part Four. But if your pup is coming very happily to his name, the instruction 'come' and your body language, he will find it very easy to associate the whistle as well.

Here's what to do. Once you are happy that puppy is very confident about knowing what the word 'come' means, then call him to you using that verbal instruction. As he starts to respond and trot towards you, just blow a gentle 'pip, pip, pip' on your whistle. Decide how many 'pips' you will use, and from now onwards, always stick to that number. The pips are a single instruction, and as with all other instructions, don't ever repeat them. This first time your puppy will more or less ignore the whistle or he might stop and look at you for a moment, so you can say his name to encourage him a bit. For the next few days repeat this exercise. Then move on to the next stage. When he is playing around, wait until his attention is on you rather than focused on something interesting elsewhere. Now blow the whistle, but don't use the verbal instruction. Get down low and give plenty of body language encouragement to help him get the idea. You will be surprised at how quickly your pup gets the hang of this. There seems to be something compelling about the sound of the whistle, and many pups have an instinctive reaction to come automatically to the pip of the whistle with little or no training. For the next few weeks play around with all the different ways you have of asking your puppy to come back

▶ *Teaching 'sit' along with the whistle*

to you. You can use a verbal instruction, a whistle command, or body language gestures. Sometimes use one and sometimes use another – or use them in combination. With young pups I spend a lot of time using the whistle in combination with patting my thighs and having a low body position. Do remember to use these visual, body language cues at least as often as you use the other types of instruction. Many dogs get a little bit deaf in their old age (it's not always just an excuse!) and that's when your visual signals will come in handy.

When the puppy is older and his formal training begins, you will be asking for a really very precise response to the whistle command, without any support from either verbal or visual back-up. But for now, the whole thing is just a game, so don't attempt to achieve too much. At this stage, only introduce the 'come' whistle. The other whistle instructions can be taught when the puppy is older. When he is still six months or younger, it is too confusing for him to try to do too much. If he doesn't obey the whistle command, don't repeat it and don't make any other kind of fuss. Just go back to using verbal instructions for a couple of days, and then begin again with the whistle. The penny will drop eventually.

◀ *Teaching 'come' combined with the whistle 'pip, pip, pip'*

Introduce the collar and lead

It isn't widely understood that in the UK it is actually a legal obligation for a dog to wear a collar and be on a lead when he is in a public place. Check out the back of the book for a full rundown on all the different legislation about dogs. Hopefully you will never be bothered by legal stuff, but it's important to know all the same. So one of the first things you must get for your pup is a puppy collar with a name tag, and a clip-on lead. Although you can get puppy collars everywhere from the supermarket to online, I recommend getting your pup's first collar from the vet at the time he has his initial vaccination and check-up. There are a surprising number of pitfalls in choosing collars! Many pups, especially from the lighter-coated breeds, have very sensitive skin and can actually have allergies to the plastics used in the bottom-of-the-range collars. The fit of the collar and its width in relation to the puppy's neck length is also very important, with breeds like hounds and whippets needing specialist collars. Your vet will be able to advise about this. The name tag should be robust and non-allergenic. If you have had your pup microchipped (recommended) you will receive a collar tag with his chip details and contact number for whichever company is operating the chip scheme.

At this stage you don't need anything very special when it comes to the lead. I usually choose a colourful canvas lead with a good quality clip at one end and a loop at the other. You will almost certainly lose it, so it's probably not a good idea to get the diamante one at this point. Your puppy will grow out of this first training collar and lead very quickly, so don't be tempted to buy anything too highly technical that you may see advertised. The most important thing about the collar is that it must be comfortable for the pup, and that any pressure from him pulling against it (which he inevitably will at the beginning) is distributed evenly.

Now put the collar on! This may be a bit of a wriggly, squirmy business. Don't worry, puppy will soon get used to it, no matter what his body language may claim. I don't leave the collar on while pup is round the house, as prolonged collar wearing can damage the coat and even lead to chafing. It is good for puppy to get used to the routine of coming to you and sitting quietly in front of you while you put the collar on. Having said that, with some of the more excitable breeds, this task is not easily mastered! It can be extraordinarily frustrating trying to clip the collar on while pup is rolling around and generally turning himself inside out. Stay calm. Refuse to engage with the pup while he is being silly. Wait for him to calm down and start again. Little moments like this set the trend for your long-term training of pup. If things are getting out of hand before you've even put the collar on, it's not a good sign for an upcoming training lesson. If on the other hand, puppy is already sitting calmly and obediently to have his collar put on, that's a good indication of how things will be going forward.

First lead work lesson

If you have a garden, this is the best place for your first lead work lesson. If not, you can still do useful things just walking up and down the kitchen or in the hall. Don't be tempted to do your first lead work out in the park or in a big field where there are lots of distractions and if things go a bit pear-shaped it's harder to do something about it.

◀ *Puppy's first lead lesson*

▲ *Continuing the lead lesson*

Also don't use a road or pavement where you might get tangled up with other road users.

Put the collar on before you go out into the garden. In the garden, let puppy have a little play around and go to the loo if he needs to.

◀ *Discourage pup from jumping up at the lead by holding it short*

Then call him to you and sit him up in front of you. You already have the 'come' command; and 'sit' in front of you has been taught using the food bowl. Now you are usefully putting these two commands together and the result will be that puppy is sitting calmly and obediently in front of you, so that you can reach down and clip on the lead. This is how it should be. I must admit that isn't how it was when I had my first puppy. Instead it was more likely that I would call her a couple of times (with no result) before managing to catch her and after a brief, undignified tussle I would somehow get the lead clipped on. The aim of this book is to save you from these embarrassments and frustrations. Some of the dog training books that I have read can occasionally feel very dull and strict, with little room for you to do things your own way and enjoy your dog. I think all the time you spend with your dog should be fun. Over the years I have come to realise that it is generally more fun for both of you, if the dog basically does what he's told when you ask him to do something. The whole mad, catch-me-if-you-can routine is all very amusing at first, but when you desperately need to get the dog walked quickly so you can do the school run, it just becomes immensely stressful. So it is worth taking the time and effort to learn how to do it properly and then teaching your pup.

When you have clipped the lead on, start walking forward. If you are lucky, and have one of the calmer breeds of dog, the puppy will naturally trot alongside you. More likely though he will react to the sensation of the collar and lead. Some puppies just sit down and plant themselves, refusing to walk forward. Others dash off to play as normal and then leap about like a fish on a line when they discover the constriction of the lead. Or pup will do a combination of both, sitting in confusion for a moment before making a rush forward. Once in a while you will get a pup that turns round and tries to chew the lead. Don't let any of this bother you. Here are the things to do – they may feel pretty basic, but they work very quickly!

Pup plants himself: There's no fancy way of solving this – just drag him gently along until he gets the message and starts to walk.

Pup rushes on ahead: Again, no sophisticated solutions, just give the lead a gentle tweak to get him back alongside you.

Pup is like a mad thing: Keep walking! When you need to drag, drag; when you need to tweak, tweak, but mainly just keep walking at a gentle, steady pace while giving pup time to sort himself out and settle down to the unfamiliar way of doing things.

Pup tries to chew the lead: This can become an irritating little habit, so nip it in the bud. Have pup walking very close to you and hold the lead quite short with your hand in a line directly above pup's head. This means that he can't twist round to bite at the lead. As long as he doesn't get away with it, he will soon give up trying.

Pup keeps putting his paws over the top of the lead: This is another annoying trick certain breeds can develop if the lead has been too slack in their early lessons. Working dogs that don't do a lot of training on or with the lead are very prone to it, and I have seen top professional trainers carry a fully grown small dog for miles rather than keep having to untwine it from the lead. Use the same remedy as for chewing. Even if your dog is eventually aimed at various working or competition activities and won't be spending much time on the lead, do bother to train him properly. In competitions he will need to be on the lead sometimes and it is extremely irritating to spend hours constantly untwining your dog from his lead.

Pup seems really upset: If pup is genuinely rather scared by the lead he will show it by weeing or pooing or whining or shaking his head. This is a sign that it is too soon for him to be doing much with the lead. Keep on getting him used to his collar. Clip the lead on in the house and let him run round with him just trailing it behind him for a few minutes. Supervise this so that he doesn't get caught up on it or start chewing it. Then gradually get back to the point where you are walking forward holding on to the lead. Things change very fast with young pups, so it may only be a matter of days before he is ready to deal with the lead.

Walking on the lead

Once you have pup to the point where he will more or less trot alongside you without too much madness, start doing a few little lead exercises. At this stage it is simply a matter of walking slowly and steadily at a regular pace that is easy for your pup to keep up with. Walk in little circles and loops and go this way and that, so that pup has to think about where you are going and pay attention to you rather than just messing around with the lead. This lesson should always be short. To begin with, just do a couple of minutes. As pup gets older you can extend it to five minutes or so. Later on, when you are doing heeling and lead work training, the lesson will be longer and will include all sorts of little on-the-lead training tasks. With a young pup, it's plenty just to be at the stage where he accepts the lead and trots along happily by your side.

Understand the true connection between you and your dog

It may not seem like it, but putting on the lead is actually a big step in the relationship between you and your growing-up puppy. With readers who come to me for advice, I have begun to realise that the function of the lead is really misunderstood by even quite experienced dog owners. Everybody assumes that the lead is a connection between you and your puppy. It's easy to see why we would think this: after all, the lead is essentially a piece of string tying you and your dog together.

Now look at it another way. The lead is actually something that comes in between you and your dog. Before you first put that lead on, you and your puppy had a connection that was so strong you didn't need to be physically tied together. If you wanted to communicate with each other you used body language, eye contact, vocalisation – and it worked. So why now communicate with each other by this Stone Age method of tugging a piece of string?

The lead is a fact of life. You need to know how to use the lead for safety (mainly your dog's safety) and because the law says so. But the lead is not the best method of communicating with and guiding your dog. Don't fall into the trap that I see so many times, of using the lead as a substitute for a real, meaningful partnership with your dog. My dogs are pretty obedient and live in the countryside half a mile from the nearest public road, so the dogs and I are very lucky that we never have to use a lead from one week's end to the next. Our relationship is all the better for it, because there is nothing coming between us. If I ask them to heel, or come, or sit, or stay, or go away, they will do that because they are happy to cooperate with my instruction, not because I have yanked them off their paws or have them tied to a long piece of bungee elastic.

So the lead is something we all have to use for trotting along the road, or in a public place, or during certain activities. It is not a short cut to controlling your dog without training. Even worse are the dog owners who get into a kind of nuclear arms race with their dog about the lead. They start with an ordinary lead, but the pup starts pulling so they get some kind of head halter, but that doesn't work either, so then it's on with the body harness. In the end the poor old dog might just as well be pulling a cart he's got so many straps and stuff on him. And remember – the larger breeds of dog are more than capable of pulling a cart. The more harnesses you put on him, the easier you make it for him to get his body weight into the pulling. The daughter of a friend had four front teeth knocked out by a Labrador in a harness who pulled her into the kerb so fast she was snapped flat on her face.

Retractable elastic leads are also problematic. Usually you see them being used by people whose dogs are too badly behaved to be allowed free play. The retractable lead gives the dog a little more freedom than an ordinary lead, but it is still cruel to deny a dog access to free movement simply because you cannot be bothered to build a partnership with him. I'm sorry if this sounds blunt, but please take a moment to think about it. Look at your little four- or five- or six-month-old puppy playing around happily at your feet. Are you really comfortable about a scenario where he spends the next fourteen years of his life going out tied to a piece of elastic? I thought not. Keep reading this book for how to avoid that.

The children's chapter

At this stage of his life your pup is learning through your consistent guidance rather than any formal training, and much of what you are showing him is discovered through play. The best thing possible just now is for puppy to be able to take these few basic, but fundamental, ideas on board without any worries, and for them to become deeply embedded. You can recruit your children to help you do this! During child–puppy playtime, your children can play the kind of little games with pup that will help him and your children to learn at the same time. So if your children are interested in puppy (need I ask!), then you can get them involved.

Puppy playtime with your children shouldn't be more than fifteen minutes, once or twice a day. Supervise them the first few times, and

▲ *As puppy gets older, everyone can join in the fun – even Mr Snowman!*

generally keep an eye out. Remind your children about the ground rules discussed so far in the book. Now here are some learning games they can play together.

Hide and seek: You keep puppy distracted while your child goes and hides somewhere within hearing of the puppy (this can be played in the house or in the garden). Then your child has to guide the puppy to her by using his name or the whistle or any other sound, but not the word 'come'. This is a great exercise for the puppy in learning to find the caller, and by banning the instruction 'come' you make the game more fun as well as avoiding the risk of misusing or over-using the word 'come'.

The maze: Either in the house or the garden, you and your child construct a path winding through various obstacles like cushions, chairs, flower pots, etc. Now your child puts pup on the lead and has to lead him through the path without touching any of the obstacles. This is good for teaching the puppy about the lead.

Statues: The main form of this game involves you as well as your child. Your child and puppy are playing or wandering around the room or the garden and you say 'sit'. Your child has to stop instantly and stand still, and also ask the puppy to sit. There are lots of different versions of this game. When the puppy is older you can make it that you blow a 'stop' command on the whistle and both child and puppy have to stop instantly, with the first one to stop being the winner. Don't overdo the game though, never more than three 'sits' at a time.

Buried body: Your child hides a couple of pup's toys (never more than two) and then helps him find them. Don't repeat this game too often, or the puppy may get stale.

Trackers: This is a version of buried body using a scent trail, and it can be very interesting to watch. Get something with plenty of human smell on it like an old sock or a glove or a vest. Keep the puppy where he can't see and let your child lay a short trail by dragging the item along the ground or over furniture up to the place where the item is then hidden. Then the pup has to follow the scent trail. A lot of pups won't really manage this and will generally bumble around before goofing across the hidden item – but it is fascinating to watch the occasional pup who has a natural nose for following a trail.

Football: This is a version of a fetching game and is best played in the garden rather than the house. Either roll or kick a tennis ball gently along the ground for pup to go and fetch and get it back to you as best he can. Then kick it over to your child for them to roll or kick for the puppy again. A good pup will get there first and get the tennis ball before your child can, rather in the way that any team can beat England at football. Don't play it for too long. All these games need to be really special for pup so that he stays interested.

Warning about fetch games: The game most commonly played with pups and young dogs is chucking a stick for him to catch and bring back. This is really quite dangerous. Every year vets see a great many dogs with severe injuries from trying to catch pointy sticks – some dogs even die from stick-catching injuries. It also jazzes up your young dog and makes him overexcited to the point where you lose control. If you are interested in 'fetch', or retrieving as it is known professionally, and your pup likes it too, then why not plan to make that an activity to train your dog for? Doing retrieving in a structured way is far more interesting, so look out for the sections about it later in the book.

▲ *Any favourite toy can be used to play training games*

This is a simple checklist to make sure everything is going to plan by the time puppy has reached approximately six months old.

- Pup clearly knows his boundaries

- Recognises the difference between right and wrong

- Is well socialised – remains relaxed and well behaved when meeting new humans/dogs

- Knows the 'big four little words': *name, come, sit, no*

- Obeys the 'big four' 90 per cent of the time

- Is aware of the whistle even if not quite understanding it

- Calmly allows you to put collar and lead on

- Walks on the lead

Frequently Asked Questions about three months to six months

Q. Why should I be doing so much with the puppy when he is still so young?

A. Many first-time puppy owners are told: 'oh don't worry about training; let him enjoy his puppyhood and then start training when he is about six to eight months old.' There are two issues here. First of all, many experienced dog owners are training their puppy far more than they realise from the very beginning, even if they don't call what they are doing 'training'. Which leads to the second issue: what do we mean by the word 'training'? Toilet training is understood, but when does playing hide and seek become training your dog to come?

A lot of people ask me, 'when should I start training my pup?' to which my reply is: 'both now and never'. In other words, your puppy will be learning as soon as he arrives home, but you never want it to feel like hard work and formal training for the pup. You are aiming for everything to be absorbed very naturally. This is one of the reasons for starting with small learning games right from the beginning, when it is absolutely instinctive for the pup to look to you for guidance and to learn from you without questioning. If you leave your pup to run completely wild until he is six or eight months old, it will make life difficult. He will already have worked out his own way of doing things – which almost certainly won't coincide with yours. And instead of a gentle increase in the challenge of what you are asking him to do, he will suddenly be faced with a load of things he knows nothing about. It's a bit like sending a child to secondary school without having taught him how to read or write.

So it's a good idea to start now, but if you are still getting the feeling you are asking too much of your puppy, then take a few steps backward. If he seems confused by anything, just give him more time. Give him plenty of mental and physical rest. Don't keep pushing your pup. You'll soon start getting signals that he is stale or bored.

Q. My puppy used to sit fine when he was little and now he doesn't do it any more

A. This is a really common problem with puppies making the transition from early puppyhood to being young dogs, and it is usually as a result of us becoming complacent! When teaching the pup to sit to begin with using the feed bowl, pups catch on really quickly. Then we teach the sit at other times without the feed bowl, and that goes well too, so we assume that the lesson has been learned and we don't need to bother with it any more. So it's very tempting not to bother with the feed bowl sit any more, and then, before you know it, achieving the sit at other times becomes harder. So be scrupulous about the feed bowl sit, and always do it – even late into the dog's life.

It is the same case with a lot of lessons that pup learns early and easily. They have a tendency to become sloppy as new training is introduced. So make a point of going back and doing 'revision' every so often. Never let those big four words slip. It is all too easy not to notice that you have got into the habit of saying 'come' more than once, so keep checking up!

Q. The puppy is constantly getting upstairs and weeing on the bed

A. This presupposes that you don't want the puppy upstairs. If you do want the puppy upstairs, then the occasional accident on the bed is almost inevitable. But if puppy is getting into the bedroom when he's not meant to, then the wee on the bed is almost certainly out of anxiety because the pup has realised that he's got into this place where he's not really meant to be. With a very dominant pup it can also be a bit of a power play: 'Look I own this bed now!' In either case, the answer is fairly straightforward. Had you considered shutting the bedroom door? Or putting a gate at the bottom of the stairs? Or putting pup in his pen when you can't supervise his play? I can imagine any number of six-month-old pups who, if they could, would write to ask me: 'I'm so worried about my human, she keeps leaving the bedroom door open, and I've no idea whether I'm meant to be in there or not?'

Q. My puppy is a bit snappy and barking with strangers when we are out in the park

A. In their early socialising, pups often go through a phase of being a bit insecure and defensive with strangers. Don't rush into going nuclear and getting into a punishment scenario, which is likely to make the pup feel even more anxious. Instead take the pressure off by backing down on the socialising a bit. Concentrate instead on your at-home work. Make sure the puppy has a really reliable, consistent routine. He needs to feel secure in himself, and the more predictable life is, the easier he will find it. Then gradually reintroduce the socialising in low pressure situations. If he is small enough, you can carry him when necessary. If he is bigger, make sure he is on the lead and that you don't have the lead too slack. Talk to him soothingly and reassuringly and use physical contact with him. Let him back off a little from the stranger. Explain to the other person that you are puppy socialising. Sometimes you will find yourself meeting another dog person that way and you end up chatting in such a relaxed way that pup takes his cue from you and relaxes as well. Try to keep calm, even if you are feeling a bit worried. Take the heat out of the situation by communicating pleasantly. So don't scream 'Stay away from my dog, you're scaring him.' Instead say quietly, 'Good morning, I'm so sorry about the way my dog is behaving. He's very young and not used to strangers, but he will calm down in a moment.'

Q. I think there is something wrong with my puppy, sometimes he behaves perfectly, and other times he won't do anything I ask.

A. This conundrum does pop up occasionally. Sometimes pups go through a kind of teenage phase, and bitches especially can be a bit moody when they have their first 'season' (*oestrus*) at around eight months old. Usually all you need to do is persist calmly and things will get better. Be aware though, that if you have the type of Artful Dodger puppy described at the beginning of the chapter, you could face a fair amount of this difficult behaviour in the early stages. But if you persist with the training, and are really firm about boundaries and your leadership, he should gradually come round to your way of thinking.

Rather more difficult to solve is the puppy behaving in this inconsistent way because *you* are being inconsistent yourself. Reread Part Two of this book and you will begin to understand about why so much emphasis is put on your own personality as the person training the dog. If you are moody and erratic, your dog will grow up insecure and confused. If you don't show leadership, your dog will grow up disrespectful. Ultimately you can't change your whole personality in order to train your puppy, but just being aware of your personal strengths and weaknesses can make a huge difference. And when training a young pup, you can certainly influence the kind of dog he grows up to be.

Q. My puppy is pulling really hard on the lead. Should I get a harness?

A. The original purpose of a harness, both for horses and dogs, was to make it easier for the animal to use its whole body weight to pull something, so you can see that it would be quite illogical to get a harness if you are having trouble holding your pup on the lead. Most lead pulling problems come from the dog owner not being firm and decisive about stopping the pup from pulling. Obviously the pup is going to pull and mess around the first couple of times while he is still getting used to the lead. If he continues to pull after that, the solution is simple. One very firm jerk on the lead – pretty much hard enough to pull him off his paws – and he will stop. He may start pulling again, just to see if the big jerk was a mistake. When he finds out that pulling ends up with him off his paws, he will stop. It is important to put a stop to the pulling while the pup is still young enough for you to be successful. If he gets larger, he may get too strong. The surprise element is more important than the physical one, so the jerk must come as a bolt from the blue – not the end of a long pulling battle. When you jerk, say 'Ach, ach, NO' very firmly. Don't worry that you are hurting the pup. Any pup that can pull that hard is tough enough to be caught up firmly. Don't get into an eternal pulling battle.

Timid, novice dog owners being pulled all over the place by their dogs is a very common sight in our streets and parks. It is a sign that the dog is on top, not just in this matter, but throughout his relationship with his owner. So if you are having this problem, it's time to man up a bit and be firm.

Q. The children love the puppy, but they want to play with him all the time.

A. Puppies need shorter playtimes than children, so it can be difficult while the pup is still new to the family and the children are besotted with him. However, there are lots of other puppy-related activities that the children can get involved in without actually having to bother the puppy. How about taking photos of him while he's sleeping and uploading them onto the computer to create a puppy Facebook page? Or doing paintings and drawings of puppy? Older children can get involved in planning puppy's training and keeping a log of what he has done so far. Dog blogs written by your child on behalf of the pup are a great way of getting your child interested in all sorts of new writing and creative skills.

PART THREE: SUMMARY

PUPPY FROM THREE MONTHS TO ABOUT SIX MONTHS

In the last three months your puppy will have been learning very quickly, and maturing to the point where he can cope with more serious training. Here's a quick reminder of the things covered in this section.

Puppy Personality Profiler
Obedience
Socialising
The Big Four Little Words
The Whistle
The Collar and Lead
The Children's Chapter
Puppy's Key Stage One
Frequently Asked Questions

Now puppy is a bit more grown-up and has learnt the basics, it's time to do some more formal training. Part Four will tell you all you need to know to bring up your pup to be a well-behaved, fully trained young dog at around a year old.

PART FOUR

'BIG SCHOOL' TRAINING FROM ABOUT SIX MONTHS

As he reaches the age of about six months your puppy will be flying! He's growing up and maturing quickly, and this is an age where he can learn very rapidly. The basic training and socialising you have already done has helped form the basis of a great partnership with your pup. Now it's time to build on that by introducing some more formal training. Part Four takes you through the next six months or so of serious training to help your pup be a well-behaved, obedient and trained young dog at around a year old.

▶ *An old soft dummy is easier for a youngster*

The partnership – wanting the same thing

Forget what lots of dog training manuals and professional dog handlers may tell you – in fact, dog training is easy! There is a big secret to training your pup successfully, and it is very simple. If your dog already wants to do what you are asking him to do, then he will do it. Just think about it. If a friend asks you to have a cup of coffee or a chocolate, are you going to disobey them? It would be terribly rude to say no, and of course, you'd love a cup of coffee or a chocolate

▶ *Patiently waiting for the 'all dogs run round madly' command*

anyway! So that invitation, or command, is pushing on an open door. It is the same with your dog. As a joke for my friends I sometimes sit my tribe of spaniels up in front of me for a while, before firmly issuing the instruction: 'All dogs run around madly!' I can guarantee that is one command that is always understood and never disobeyed. So if your dog understands what you want him to do, and he wants to do it as well, then your training programme will be problem-free. All we need to do now is make sure that the dog can understand what we are asking, and that we have created a context where he does want to do it too.

◀ *Instantly obeying the 'all dogs run round madly' command*

Understanding

If all has been going well between you and your pup for the last six months, by now you and he will have a good understanding of each other. One of the main aims of the early instructions we give our pup – like 'sit' and 'come' – is to teach him our language. His obedience in those first few months is somewhat less important than him learning to 'speak human'. If your puppy passed his Key Stage One happily, then he has enough vocabulary in place to be able to understand what you will ask him as his training progresses. If he struggled with Key Stage One, it would be a good moment to backtrack a bit and revise before you get started on this section.

By now you too should have a pretty good understanding of your puppy! The Puppy Personality Profiler will have helped you discover a lot about his underlying character, which will give you clues about how he will respond to his future training. You will also both be reading each other's body language. You will recognise the signs that he is confused or anxious or tired or in a boisterous mood. And your puppy will know better than you realise what kind of mood you are in. He will be able to tell if you are feeling stressed or happy and whether or not it is a good moment to take the mickey. Remember though, that you need to be able to control your mood when you are training. Be aware of it yourself. If you are already cross about something else, definitely don't have a training session until you are feeling calmer. Equally, if you are happy for non-puppy-related reasons you must make sure your dog doesn't spot this. He may take advantage of your good mood. Given that you are understanding each other reasonably well, the next really important platform for the ongoing training is that you both want the same thing – that you have mutual objectives.

We want the same thing

The technical phrase for creating a shared goal with you dog is 'behaviour modification'. This simply means that left to himself, your dog would already be doing more or less what you are about to ask him to do, and therefore it comes much more easily. As trainers, what we are seeking to do is 'modify' our dog's existing behaviour, rather than impose a brand new set of rules and actions on him. This process was how domestication of dogs began. In the wild, packs of dogs work together to separate a prey animal from its herd and then bring it down. You will probably have seen something similar on wildlife programmes showing African wild dogs or even hyenas cutting out a young wildebeest from its group; or wolves chasing elk. So man didn't have to do very much training at all to produce what we would recognise as a sheep dog. It is the same with huntingdogs, which are used to retrieve birds that have been shot for eating. It is a natural instinct for wild dogs to scavenge dead animals and bring them back to the pack, so in domestication, we were working with established behaviours.

Nowadays we don't all want our dogs to herd sheep or retrieve birds (although of course these activities continue) but we do want them to come when we call; to behave well; and to take part in a variety of activities. So we have to create a context for our training where those are the things the dog wants to do, just as much as we want him to do them. He should want to come when we call because it means something nice is about to happen – which might be play or physical contact or reward. He will enjoy behaving well and won't perceive it as a chore, but just a natural part of his happy, relaxed life and personality. Taking part in a variety of activities is something which most dogs enjoy anyway, and all we need to do is teach them the language and structure of those activities. One of my spaniels, Ricky, was a 'guinea-pup' for my first book about dogs, *Training the Working Spaniel*, and he's now a grown-up dog. I'm very proud of him because I'm always being complimented on what a lovely personality he has. With Ricky, I concentrated very carefully from the beginning on creating a training environment where he was never conscious of it being an effort to do what I asked. So now, as a grown-up dog, it is his pleasure to sit attentively and wait for me to finish whatever I am doing, even if it means being patient for thirty or forty minutes. And he always gives me a bunch of flowers on Valentine's Day (though he hasn't worked out how to buy them yet).

'Big school' training from about six months

▶ *Ricky is the only male who can be relied on for flowers on Valentine's Day*

Opening the door

An important aid to setting your mutual agenda is making sure that the door is already at least partly open. In Part Two we had a look at the various different types and breeds of dogs and their original functions and current strengths. Knowing this is an important part of training. If you want to train your dog to be steady and patient sitting around the home for long periods of time, it will be much more difficult to do this with a very active, go-getting working breed. Conversely, if you are planning to train your dog to do lots of activities with you, it would suit a working breed much better. A mastiff has a natural (and to an extent, inbred) behaviour that is completely different from that of a Labrador. Put at its simplest: if you want a guard dog, don't choose a Labrador; if you want a fun, family dog that visitors can play with, don't choose a mastiff. So, look at the breed and type of dog you have and be aware of what is going to come naturally to him and what isn't. Obedience and loyalty come naturally to a Labrador – flyball competition or burglar-chasing does not! The dogs that we admire, that form the closest bonds with their humans, are those where the team of human and dog have exactly the same agenda.

Adjusting your agenda

Through getting to know your pup and his breed/type, you can get a good idea of what his agenda is. If it is exactly the same as yours, it's plain sailing. But even in perfect partnerships there have to be compromises on both sides. Your dog will not want to be as obedient as you want him to be, and he has to take that on board. Equally, he may want more stimulation and activity (and general full-on mud) than you do, and you have to adjust for that. This is how you reward each other. You reward your dog by getting down and dirty with him from time to time, and he rewards you by being obedient when you tell him it matters. Like any relationship, it will inevitably involve a little 'give and take'.

Praise and reward

One of the most obvious ways we create a climate of both dog and human wanting the same thing is through the use of praise and reward. If you have a slightly different agenda from what your dog's instinctive agenda would be, you are going to have to use reward more than if you have exactly the same agenda. If the dog wants to do it, then being allowed to do it is its own reward. For example, Ricky absolutely adores retrieving and loves to go and find or fetch anything and everything and bring it back to me. The expression on his face as he joyfully discovers a manky old dead frog or similar and rushes back to me with this delightful gift, is unmistakeable in dog or human language. So when I am working with Ricky or training him, I know that the best possible reward I can give him is to let him go off and retrieve something for me. Since this actually happens to be his job in daily life, everyone is happy! Even if I'm training him to do something else, I can still give him the opportunity to have a retrieve as his big reward at the end of the lesson, so I don't need to give him a food treat or anything like that.

When you are training a dog slightly outside his comfort zone or to do a job that he wasn't born for, then just doing the job won't be enough of a reward in itself. As you get to know your pup, you will work out which of the rewards works best for him. Here are the five main rewards most often used.

Rewards:

1. *Verbal praise* – by far the best and most obvious of all the rewards. It is instant, you can do it at a distance and you don't have to remember to bring it with you. When your dog has done exactly what you have asked him to do, use a lovely, warm voice to tell him 'Good dog, well done,' and his name. Remember to make your praise voice very different from your telling-off voice. And don't use praise unless your dog is definitely doing what you want. If you praise him when he is misbehaving you are just plain pleading with him. It is so embarrassing to hear people basically begging their dog to do as he's

told: 'Come here; good dog; there's a good boy; come...' when there's nothing good about it.

2. *Doing the job* – for most working dogs being trained to do a job, just being allowed to do the job is all the reward they need. If your dog is going to be working on retrieving, then a single retrieve at the end of a lesson is the ideal reward. For dogs in any working disciplines, at the end of the training session you can set up a small, working scenario for them to succeed at. It should be a little bit easier than what you have just been training them to do, so that they will achieve it easily and get canine satisfaction as a result.

3. *Physical affection* – another very simple and instinctive way of rewarding your dog. At the end of an agility run you will see dogs jumping into their owners' arms for a big, fun cuddle. Dogs are very physical and paws-on, and they communicate physically as much as they do verbally, so physical rewards work really well. Different dogs like to be touched in different ways. Some love to have their tummies rubbed. Others prefer a full-on jump up and being allowed to lick you. More serious dogs prefer just to have their muzzles rubbed or head stroked. Find out what your pup likes best so you can be ready to reward him with it after he has done well. Be careful with more excitable breeds though, as too much physicality can send them over-the-top quite quickly. Save it for the end of the lesson. With my cockers, all praise while the lesson is going on is quite muted, otherwise things can get a bit hyper.

4. *Food treats* – many dog trainers use food treats, and you can see people training for obedience and heel work with little hipster bags to keep their food treats in. These are sometimes also combined with 'clicker training' where the click of the clicker marks the successful behaviour which is then reinforced with the food treat. As a dog owner I have to admit that I find this all a bit of a rigmarole. It just doesn't come naturally to me to remember to click and have a treat hidden in my hand, etc., when instinctively all I want to do is say 'Good boy', and give his neck a rub. Plus, since I can barely remember my dog lead or even my car keys when going out training, having to take a little bag

of treats and a clicker is just too much for me! The less clobber I have when going training, the more natural the learning process. Just pottering along a field edge or footpath with barely even a lead, you can teach your dog to watch you and focus on you with all his attention. I want him to be obsessed with me, not what I might have in a bag round my waist. In all my training, I am trying to achieve a close, natural bond between me and my dog. I want my dog to do as I ask because he lives to please me, not because he thinks he's going to get a bit of food. I feel that the food treat and/or the clicker is just another thing that comes between you and the dog. Other forms of reward are instant and personal. The only time I ever give my dog food treats is if there is a worming tablet buried in them (plus the occasional sausage from the picnic which we don't admit to). However some dogs, especially those being taught lessons which go against the grain, respond well to having some food treats as a reward. Try to avoid overdoing the food treats if you do decide to use them.

▶ Right: *An old pair of socks is one of the easiest and most useful training aids*

▶ Far right: *You can use them to keep pup's attention when teaching heeling*

5. *Object treats* – the dog's favourite possession, usually some kind of toy, is a form of reward very often used in training working dogs in the area of search and rescue and also assistance dogs. When the dog is being trained to search, he's often started by searching for his favourite toy. Then, when he has graduated to searching for other things, he's rewarded for a successful find by being given his toy. This is quite useful in general training as well. When you are teaching your pup to heel close to you and pay attention, you can keep his toy in your pocket as an additional incentive for him to focus. I usually get my young pups very keen on old pairs of socks. These smell of me (certainly to a dog's nose!) and are very convenient to roll up into a ball or pull out into a ragger. If you have a pair stuffed in your pocket, they can even double as a pair of gloves to accept that manky old dead frog I mentioned!

◀ *Or they are great for fetch exercises*

Sit, stop, stay

The reason the 'sit' is the first thing we teach our pups from day one is because it is the foundation stone for future training. A pup who is sitting obediently and attentively, focused on you, is a puppy who is ready for his lessons. The next stage is to add 'stop' and 'stay' to the 'sit'. Together these three commands will give you a platform to go on and do almost anything you want with your pup, especially in combination with the 'come' instruction. Start by making sure your original feed bowl 'sit' is still working as well as ever, and that you have arrived at the stage where pup will sit when you ask whether you have the feed bowl or not. Now we can establish the 'sit' instruction as an independent command.

▶ *You always want your dog's focus to be completely on you*

1. *Sit*

Ask your puppy to sit verbally, and at the same time raise your hand up to about eye level with your arm outstretched and the palm flat, facing slightly forwards, very much like a traffic officer stopping your car. This hand gesture is now basically replacing what you do with a feed bowl: it gets the puppy's eyes up, attentively looking at you. The main point is that it can be seen by the puppy from quite some distance. This is your visual signal for 'sit'. Do some lessons with this over the next few days. Every time you are with pup, playing or doing other lessons, use the verbal instruction 'sit', combined with your hand signal. If pup cottons on to this quickly, experiment with the pup being slightly further away from you when you give the commands. Always make sure that the puppy's attention is mainly on you when you give the instruction. Getting a successful response to a command is very much a matter of timing. If you give your command when puppy has just found a particularly interesting smell in the flower bed or is rushing off to greet your daughter, you will not get a good response (at least not until training is complete); but if you choose a moment when pup is already looking at you, or doesn't have anything better to do, then you are much more likely to get the prompt and precise obedience that you are looking for. The more often the pup obeys instantly, the more likely he is to do so in the future. Eventually he will respond even when his focus is elsewhere.

Don't repeat the instruction too often. Little five minute lessons a few times a day are the way to go. If puppy has got the message and is behaving well it is important not to make him stale by overdoing things. Play around with this over the next few days and then start to introduce the whistle. This is very much the same process as you used when teaching the 'come' to your very young pup in Part Three. You will start by adding the whistle to your other two forms of instruction, and then getting to the point where you can get your puppy to sit either to verbal, visual or whistle command.

Hold your whistle in your left hand, ready to pop into your mouth. Put up your hand in the visual sit signal at the same time as commanding 'sit' verbally, and then instantly putting the whistle in your mouth and blowing the single long 'peeeep'. The pup should already have sat before you can get your whistle blown, but that's OK. Repeat this lesson a few times over the next couple of days, and then once again, start playing around with the different combinations of the three forms of command. Gradually, the combination to concentrate on is the one where you have your hand raised in the visual signal at the same time as you blow the whistle, without using the verbal command. When you are practising this combination it helps to have your whistle already in your mouth, and to blow it at exactly the same time as you raise your hand. At first you may need to back it up a bit by spitting out your whistle and giving the verbal 'sit' command. Surprisingly quickly, though, you will find that your pup is responding to any single command or a combination. Now he's ready to go on and learn the 'stop' command – which is just the 'sit' command given at increasingly long distances.

2. Stop

Along with 'come', the 'stop' command is about the most important instruction you will ever teach your dog. A lot of dog owners don't realise it can be done, and will be amazed and impressed when you use it in the park. Being able to stop your dog and sit him on command wherever he is and whatever he is doing is absolutely vital, not just in producing a well-behaved dog, but in situations where it could genuinely be life-saving. Supposing you and the family, and of course the dog, are enjoying a country walk. He's off the lead but you suddenly realise that there are sheep running loose or a hare pops its ears up. You can stop your dog from chasing after them and getting into trouble just by blowing your stop whistle and the dog will sit and look at you immediately. Now imagine that it's not a field with sheep but a busy road with cars, and you can see how even more important it is to have a dog that instantly obeys that 'stop' command. This is especially the case for those living in urban areas where there are so many pressures on space and all sorts of unexpected situations. Teaching your dog this command properly and making sure he is obedient to it will make a huge difference to his life, because it means that it will be safe to let him off the lead where appropriate and permitted. Otherwise your urban dog could find himself spending most of his outdoor life tied up to your wrist (yes, that is essentially what a dog on the lead is experiencing).

Teaching the 'stop' follows on very naturally from the 'sit'. It is the same command, but given when the dog is at a distance. Start the process gradually.

Stage One: Short distance stop

Once your pup is 100 per cent obedient when you instruct 'sit' while he is close to you, let him go off about ten metres away and play around. Choose a moment when he already has half an eye on you. Blow the long peeep on your whistle at the same time as raising your hand. It may be necessary to reinforce by spitting out your whistle and calling, 'sit'. Your puppy will instantly sit down and look at you, ready for the next thing. Immediately **walk up to him** and give him plenty of praise.

DO NOT call him to you or let him come straight to you after the stop command. This is important. You want the pup to 'stop', not 'come'. If you wanted him to come, you would have used the 'come' instruction. But if you let him come or call him to come immediately he has stopped, then you are putting two completely different actions together into one. Very rapidly you will completely lose the 'stop' command and it will all become one to the puppy. So, as soon as the puppy has stopped and sat, you walk over to him, not the other way round.

Stage Two: Longer distances

Spend a couple of days practising your ten metre stop. As with all new lessons, don't overdo it, but introduce it in play and into other lessons. You may take pup out at this stage and have a little five or ten minutes which include playing; playing with a ball with hides and fetches; the 'come' instruction; some walking on the lead; a couple of 'stops'. When you are asking your pup to stop, try doing it at longer distances. The point of the whistle is that it can be heard further and more precisely than your voice, and you will notice this as you go to longer distances. It is the sound of the whistle that brings your pup's head up to look in your direction. He then sees your hand signal, and may hear your voice reinforcement if necessary. Remember, a puppy cannot see what he is not looking at! So there is no point waving your hand around if puppy is not actually looking at you in the first place! Whenever you are going to give a command, get the pup's attention first – and with all

▲ *Always make sure your dog's full attention is on you when giving instructions*

commands, the easiest way of doing this is with the whistle. You will soon find that you can stop your pup and have him sitting up looking at you at considerable distances. In the competitions my dogs enter it isn't uncommon for dogs to be asked to stop at 200 metres away. Don't aim for that at this stage! But you will be surprised what you can achieve. If you start having problems, just go back to the beginning and start the process all over again, gradually increasing the distance again. Always be sure that your pup is 100 per cent obedient before moving on to the next level. You need total success at the lower level in order to make sure that the more demanding level is also successful.

▲ *Use your body language when calling your dog in from a long distance*

3. *Stay*

The stay instruction is fairly obvious. It means that once he has sat down, the pup should stay sitting until you tell him to do something else. Ian Openshaw, the leading spaniel trainer in the UK, doesn't believe that 'stay' is even a command. He says that you shouldn't need to tell a really obedient pup to stay, because once the pup is sitting he won't move anyway until he gets his next instruction. Of course, logically, he's right, but for us normal dog owners, we do sometimes need the reinforcement of an extra instruction, 'stay', just to remind the puppy that he needs to concentrate on sitting still for now. You can also understand why it is important not to let pup coming rushing up to you once he has achieved the 'stop', because the point of the stop is to stop **and** wait for further instructions!

Teaching the 'stay' is simple, but can take patience. First of all, sit your pup in front of you. Hold up your hand in the 'stop' position and gradually back off a few paces away from your pup. Pup will do one of three things:

Stays put – he stays where he is, in obedience to your hand command, and because he is used to having to stay sitting when, for example, his food bowl is put down. This is great! It means that all your training has been done well, so that you have established a bond with your pup to the point that he understands what you want and is confident to do it.

▶ *Having been told to 'stay', seven-month-old Fizz settles down to wait*

Comes crawling towards you – this isn't really a big problem, but it is a sign that your puppy isn't yet confident in his relationship with you. He doesn't entirely understand you and this makes him feel a bit worried and confused, so he comes up to you for reassurance and because he thinks this might be the right thing to do.

Wanders off to do something else – this is a bad sign! It means your pup isn't really very well bonded to you or engaged with you. You must not ignore this problem, because I'm afraid it will only get worse. If a pup at only six months or so, has already got the idea that it is fine to be independent and not take any notice of you, just imagine what things are going to be like six months down the line when he is a bold, grown-up young dog. Six months doesn't seem much to a human being, but to a dog it's his whole adolescence. I'm hoping you wouldn't let your young son do exactly as he pleased throughout his teens, and it's the same with your pup. This is something you have to take on, for all your sakes. Go back a few stages with training, to the point where you have regained your pup's attention and obedience, and then start rebuilding the bond.

Corrections for stay

Spiralling – to make it easier for pup to understand that he shouldn't come over to you, you can do your moving away in a spiral, with the distance between you and the pup gradually increasing as you walk in circles around him.

Walking back – if pup begins to crawl towards you or lose concentration, then just walk quietly up to him and start again with a fresh 'sit' command. If you want to introduce the word 'stay' this would be a good time to use it. Don't use it if the pup has already got some distance towards you, because you want him to sit and stay exactly where you told him to.

Replacing – if pup comes running towards you, walk up to him and pick him up. I usually use a double handful of neck scruff to do this just to show him he's getting it wrong, but gently. Take him back to the exact spot where you stopped him (yes, you need to remember where that was, and check out the placeboard training section for more on that). Now start again with a fresh command.

Finishing the sit, stop, stay exercise

It is important to finish all training exercises clearly, so that the pup knows exactly what he's meant to be doing, and it is especially necessary to do this with sit, stop, stay. Whenever you have stopped your dog or had him staying, walk back to him before you start the next exercise or finish training. If you just let it tail off or merge into him coming back to you, then it is going to be very difficult for the dog to distinguish the 'stop' as being different from the 'come'. Stop is one of the things dogs find hardest to do, so it needs to be taught carefully and thoroughly.

At the next stage in lessons we will use sit, stop, stay alongside other instructions so that your pup will sometimes come to you after staying, and sometimes you will go to him, but get your stay established before moving on.

Perfecting come

'Come' was one of the earliest instructions you taught your puppy, and now is the time to make it part of his formal training. By now he should recognise and instantly obey the range of 'come' signals you taught him in Part Three. He should know the verbal instruction; the whistle sound 'pip, pip, pip'; and the visual signal of your hands patting your thighs and slightly crouching body language. Double-check that these all work. Is your puppy really on the spot when obeying? His response must be instant. There is a big tendency among dogs and humans to let things slide. Eighty per cent is good enough, and then 50 or 60 per cent is OK, and then before you know it, things actually aren't really happening at all. If you let it slip now, it will get worse! So patiently insist that your dog does exactly what you want at the precise moment you ask him to. If that's not happening, then backtrack and start again from where things started to go off course a bit.

Corrections for come

If you are having difficulties, first of all remember always to ask your pup to come at a moment when his attention is on you. You may be holding his favourite toy, or he may be expecting dinner time. This way we are once again pushing on that open door. We want to get the pup into the mental habit of 'oh, yes, come, I always come when I hear that.' For a timid or slightly confused pup it can be helpful to jog backwards away from him for a few strides, bringing his chase instinct into play. If he still insists on ignoring you, just go over to him and grab him and drag him towards you, while saying 'come'. No need to be nasty about it, just firm. One of the big mistakes many first-time dog owners make is to wait until the pup has finally come back and then tell him off. Think logically about this. If you tell him off when he comes back, you are effectively telling him off for coming back, i.e. for obeying the instruction. But this can leave you in a quandary. How do you tell off a naughty pup who isn't coming back promptly? I remember puzzling over this after reading the first dog training book I ever bought. The book advised rattling a rolled-up newspaper over the head of a disobedient puppy. In the middle of the North Downs, with a pup who liked to be naughty at a distance from you of about a hundred metres, I have to tell you, this piece of advice was a complete non-starter. So remember Mohammed and the mountain? If your dog won't come to you, then you must go to your dog. This is a great discipline for you as a trainer. The prospect of having to sprint a hundred metres or so through open countryside to correct a dog who is misbehaving concentrates your training mind wonderfully. It gives you a great incentive to teach the command thoroughly at home so that things never get to the mad dash through the mud stage!

Set up a controllable situation where it is easy for you to take action if the pup disobeys. The back garden is an obvious place. Check that you have the pup's attention. Ask him to 'come' and say his name. If he deliberately ignores you, then instantly descend on him and grab him and pull him over to you. You should only need to do this once, and if you have established the 'come' properly when he was younger, it is very unlikely you should ever need to do it all.

If you have a genuinely naughty youngster – perhaps an Artful

Dodger – there is another training trick you can use, which requires a friend. Again, set up a controllable situation, but this time you need it to include somewhere for your friend to hide, perhaps behind a tree or even a garden chair. Wait until pup is not far from your hidden friend and then call pup to come. When he doesn't come this is the moment for your friend suddenly to appear from behind the bush and grab pup. Pup will be amazed and think that the boss can be in more than one place at once – which usually has a very chastening effect!

EXERCISES USING COME, SIT, STOP AND STAY

Once you have all four individual elements: 'come'; 'sit'; 'stop'; 'stay' firmly in place and your puppy definitely understands and obeys the instructions, now you can start combining them all in various learning exercises, in what is the first grown-up training for your pup. As you get used to the commands you can mash them up in all sorts of ways. Here are some example exercises for you to try.

1. *Sit to come* – sit pup down and walk at least fifty metres from him before turning round, making eye contact and instructing him to come using just the whistle. This is an absolute basic for the well-behaved dog, often known as the recall, and you see it used all the time in many different dog activities and competitions, especially obedience work. It's really easy and automatic for most pups, but don't overuse it in training as it can make the pup start to anticipate the command so that the moment you have sat him down, he's already running in towards you before you've had time to give the instruction. I would only practise once for every other eight or nine exercises I do. Fortunately it doesn't need much practise.

2. *Come to stop* – as in the first exercise, sit your pup down and walk at least fifty metres from him before turning and using the come whistle. Keep the whistle in your mouth, and this time, just as the puppy is nearly halfway to you, blow the stop whistle and use the stop gesture. When the pup stops, walk up to him and give gentle praise to complete the exercise. Some puppies get this immediately, and skid to a stop, but most will be a bit confused and carry on towards you regardless. This is one of the few times where it is OK to repeat the command. Do so, and at the same time take a firm stride towards your pup and make your body language big and forbidding. This usually stops him, but if not, keep walking towards him and then give him the stop command while standing near him. This is a tough exercise for a pup who is set on his way towards you, joyfully responding to the come instruction, only to find himself stopped in his tracks. But once you have got this one cracked, then you know you really do have a young dog you can trust. Beware of getting into the habit of using the stop command more than once as the pup is running back. Once he has learnt the exercise, he must stop the first time you ask him. If it gets sloppy, you are basically losing the command altogether. Always remember to complete the exercise properly by walking up to where pup has stopped and praising him, rather than letting him carry on back to you.

3. *Come to stop to come* – the extension of the exercise above, once the puppy has stopped, is to use the come command to instruct him to continue on back to you. This is really quite advanced level, but as long as you are very clear and take it slowly and gradually, most puppies catch on very quickly. Ultimately you can see the top dog trainers use the combination of stop and come commands to move their dogs round into a precise position required by competition or work. For the time being though, just use this come, stop, come exercise from time to time as a way of checking that your pup is absolutely precise and obedient in his reaction to your instructions. Don't allow the exercise to degenerate to the point where the pup is just coming on in to you with a kind of brief stop in the middle.

4. *Come to stop to stay* – this is a really good exercise for knowing that your dog is concentrating on you. Call him to come and stop him as before. This time leave him staying in his stop position while you gradually walk round him in a large circle. Then walk up to him to praise and complete the exercise. He should stay in position even though you have moved. Some pups will try to come to you as soon as

they see you move. Just use the normal procedure of walking up to him and gently but firmly putting him back in his position. Rather comically a lot of pups will stay in position, but tie themselves in knots trying to keep eye contact with you as you walk round them. This behaviour is very encouraging for you as a trainer because it shows the lengths your pup will go to in order to keep his bond with you.

5. *Stay to come* – Sit your dog up and walk away from him about twenty to fifty metres. Circle to and fro one way and then the other. This time complete the exercise by asking your pup to come to you. Do this exercise less frequently than others so that the pup doesn't get into the habit of coming.

6. *Sit to stay with distractions* – this is a very important exercise, especially for urban dogs. Sit him up and walk away as in the previous exercises. This time you are going to perform various distractions and you want him to stay in position no matter what. Distractions can include messing around with his favourite toy. Or you can turn your back on him – this is where you learn to develop eyes in the back of your head – or if you have the opportunity you can hide. Some trainers actually pop back into the house and grab a cup of tea while their pup is sat waiting! What you are doing is teaching your pup that no matter what happens, he must continue to follow orders. Oddly enough, the most tempting distraction of all is for you to sit or lie down on the ground. This will bring all but the best behaved of pups bounding towards you. To this day some of my grown-up dogs who should know better can't resist the temptation to come rushing up and pile in if I am sitting on the ground, perhaps having a picnic, and if for no other reason, this makes this exercise important!

7. *Come to stop to stay to come* – as with the above exercise, this lesson is putting everything together in a way that you will be able to use for the rest of your dog's life, whether it is just messing around in the park or whether you intend to do more formal activities. If you can get this exercise spot on, you will be able to do most things together. Let your puppy get a good long way from you – at least fifty metres – while he is playing around. By this time you shouldn't need to worry too much about how much attention the pup has on you. He should be obedient to the come instruction in all conditions, so blow your come whistle and use your hand signal. Pup will be coming bounding towards you. Stop him midway as before. This time leave him sat while you wander about and eventually walk into a completely different position, and now instruct him to come to you in your new position. If your puppy waltzes through this first time, then you know your training is going really well.

Retrieving/fetching

Almost all dogs instinctively like to play fetch games, whether they belong to one of the retriever breeds or not. Whether you have a Chihuahua or a purpose-bred Labrador retriever, fetch games are worth teaching. While formal retrieving work is a major element in competitions and activities for working dogs, the role it plays for family dogs is more important than you might think. Along with being fun for all concerned, and great exercise, retrieving is excellent mental stimulation and a wonderful way to take your obedience training to quite an advanced level without pup ever realising he is doing anything but playing. So far you have been rolling tennis balls for your pup and letting him bring them back. You've also been playing finding games where you hide his favourite objects and let him find them and bring them back. As the puppy grows up, you have probably started throwing balls for him and letting him chase out after them. Is it also just possible you are beginning to get slightly fed up with pup's obsessive need to go and fetch and then beg you to throw again? Dogs can very quickly get compulsive about retrieving to the extent that it becomes a behaviour problem and damages other aspects of their training and obedience.

So retrieving has to step up from being just a game to a bit of a science – and you will be surprised at all the interesting lessons you can teach with just a tennis ball and couple of training dummies, like those made by Air Kong (see appendix for details). Remember that even when he is retrieving, your pup's basic obedience, including 'sit, stop, stay' must be as good as ever. So if you throw something, he's not allowed to go rushing after it until you give him a verbal command to do that – usually 'fetch'. It's also important to stop throwing the very straightforward fetches for your pup as it will overexcite him and make him more likely to be disobedient. Instead, teach your pup the exercises below and you will find that his obedience, concentration and focus on you will improve dramatically.

▶ *Using body language to send the pup to fetch a retrieve*

Dogs that play with their owners in these more complex ways form the closest of all partnerships. Try the exercises below; all you need is a couple of tennis balls and two or three training dummies.

1. *Leave to retrieve* – this is a core exercise used by professional trainers, yet it is extremely simple to teach even to a young pup. Find some kind of narrow path or green lane or the long edge of your garden where it is safe to train pup and there is a very clear straight line to

◀ *'Leave that' means the pup will wait to fetch the dummy until asked*

prevent him wandering off. Have your pup walking alongside you on the lead, or once you have taught him to heel (see below), you can have him heeling alongside you. At first though, I recommend keeping him on the lead just in case he gets a bit excited. Sit him up and throw a dummy up in the air so it falls a few feet away from him. Hopefully he will stay sitting and won't rush after the dummy. If he does make to rush for the dummy, just stop him with the lead, and sit him down as before. The dummy isn't going anywhere, so you have plenty of time to be calm.

Now tell pup firmly 'leave that'. Turn round and walk away from the dummy, with puppy trotting alongside you. After you have walked a few feet away, turn round so you are facing the dummy, which is obviously still lying there but rather further away. Sit pup up where he can see the dummy. Take him off the lead, but keep a precautionary hold of him, just in case he anticipates you. Now give him the command 'fetch' and let him go. Make sure your body is not in his way. It helps to stand to one side of him with your feet and spare hand pointing in the direction you want him to go. Most pups will instantly rush off and collect the dummy and immediately bring it back to you. Quietly take the dummy from him and put it in your pocket or bag; put puppy back on the lead and sit him up in front you for a second to complete the exercise before giving him big praise. You can use whatever command you like for the 'fetch' – some people in the gundog world use 'get out' or 'go back'. It doesn't really matter as long as you are consistent. In achieving this exercise successfully you are teaching your pup a number of things. He must continue to be obedient, 'steady', even though something exciting is happening. He must concentrate; increase his attention span; and use his memory. All these things improve your dog's mental development and maturity, which will make him much smarter than your average dog in the park.

Not all pups will succeed in this immediately, especially if they are from breeds not usually known for retrieving. You may find your Yorkshire terrier or similar is just not interested, and if that is the case, it might be wise not to push it. A pup that genuinely doesn't have an aptitude for retrieving shouldn't be forced; there are plenty of other things to do.

More likely your pup will be interested, but not get every aspect of the exercise right first time. He may rush up and grab the dummy but then start playing with it and chucking it in the air rather than bringing it back. Be prepared for this by having your whistle in your mouth and pipping your 'come' instruction. It is likely pup will then remember to come back to you and bring the dummy with him. Or he may drop the dummy in order to come back. Don't worry. Go and pick the dummy up yourself and get him interested in it again. Let him take it from you and run alongside you for a few strides before you turn round and gently take or let him give you the dummy. Other, bold, pups may rush up and grab the dummy and run off with it without making any attempt to bring it back to you. This is why you have chosen a lane or place with an edge, to limit his options for messing around. Just blow your 'come' whistle and back off from him and he should come running to you.

You can repeat this exercise a few times, walking up and down the lane. If puppy gets it straight away, don't overdo it, and don't labour the point with a pup who is having a few difficulties. Just keep everything calm and clear and keep trying the exercise over the next few days.

2. *Two-dummy leave then retrieve* – Once pup has got the hang of the first exercise, you can introduce a second dummy. Perform the first exercise. As soon as you have received the first dummy, throw a second dummy up and to one side of you where pup can see it land. Tell him to leave it, and walk away from it back in the direction from which he fetched the first dummy. After you have gone a few metres, sit him up and send him back for the second dummy in the same way as before. You will soon be walking up and down your little lane or path with puppy whooshing out for first one dummy and then the other. The idea of this exercise is to get him to realise that whenever you say 'fetch' there is always something to fetch, even if it is a different dummy in a slightly different place. It also gives you the opportunity to increase the distances without pup losing confidence, and professionals often do this exercise with distances of more than a hundred metres. Again, don't overdo things. Two or three perfect repetitions are plenty, and if it isn't going right after three or four attempts, leave it for another day.

▲ *Getting ready to throw a tennis ball diversion while the youngster is retrieving an Air Kong*

3. *Hidden retrieve* – this exercise is what the previous exercise has been preparing your pup for. Set up a retrieve as in the first exercise. When pup brings it back, you are going to lay the second dummy, just as in exercise two, but this time you do it secretly. You can either just drop the dummy down somewhere while he is setting out to fetch the first dummy, or you can just hide it by your heel when you are praising him for delivering. Don't throw the dummy or let the puppy see it. The idea is that he should be unaware that another dummy has been laid. Now walk back down the path as normal before turning and giving the pup the 'fetch' command and a pointing hand gesture. Having been used to going back up the lane, most pups will automatically set off, even though they haven't seen the dummy being thrown. Then to their surprise and delight they will find the dummy is there after all – their first 'hidden' retrieve.

Some pups are a bit confused at first, so just step back and repeat the second exercise a couple of times before trying again. With super-bright pups though, it can be tricky getting the dummy hidden without them noticing. When I was teaching Fizz this exercise, she would inevitably find my so-called hidden dummy before I had even sent her to fetch it. If this happens, lay the dummy while the pup is going out for the first dummy with his back to you. Throw the dummy underarm some way behind you. This way the puppy won't see you, and won't immediately find the dummy when he comes back. If your puppy seems to have eyes in the back of his head and still gets the better of you don't worry too much. This exercise is only a stepping stone on the way to truly 'secret' retrieves.

4. *Full-view retrieves* – now that pup has got the idea that you don't immediately chase off after a thrown ball or dummy, you can go back to throwing some dummies out in a more open space. The idea of this exercise is to reinforce the pup's obedience, to keep him steady despite the excitement of things thrown in the air. For urban dogs this is a really important exercise. When they are out and about there are likely to be lots of tempting and distracting things going on around them. People may be kicking a ball around; children will be playing; there will be picnics and joggers and ice creams. Learning this exercise especially

teaches him that he has to behave as you want him to, no matter what the temptations. I used to walk my first pup on a footpath through the local golf course. One day a golfing gentleman managed to land his ball very near the hole, just as Tara and I were walking past the green. She immediately rushed in, retrieved the golf ball and brought it back to me. Not being a golfer, I thought it was hilarious and inquired whether there was a special rule to cover this eventuality. The golfer was not amused at all – I got the impression it was one of the best shots he'd ever played! So there are excellent reasons for teaching your dog self-control.

With this exercise, sit your dog up and wander around him chucking various things in the air. He mustn't move. If he does, go and get him and take him back to where he was before, sitting him down again. There's no need for a big telling-off. Just a firm 'no' or 'leave that' is plenty; he'll soon cotton on. Once he's been steady while you have chucked at least four items, go round and pick three items up. Now walk back over to him and send him out to retrieve the final item with your 'fetch' command and pointing hand gesture – that's his reward for being good.

Next time, the exercise is mixed up a bit more. Throw a single retrieve in plain view. Tell the dog to leave it and then walk with him over to another position, so that the retrieve seems to be in a different place as far as the pup is concerned. Then send him. Sometimes don't send your pup for a retrieve, but go and pick it up yourself. The idea is to keep him guessing so that he must wait for your instruction and obey it, rather than just heading on out under his own steam. Just mess around with all these different things and you will soon find that your pup is loving the unpredictability of the game and having to concentrate on you to know what to do next. Never spend too long on these things though. Your pup is using his brain and can tire quite quickly.

If pup has a tendency still to rush in immediately on a retrieve, put him on the lead. Sit him up with the lead trailing on the ground. Just as you throw the dummy, quietly tread on the lead so that he gets brought up short when he attempts to run off.

5. *Secret retrieves* – This is your chance to get the drop on your super-smart pup. Without having your pup with you (leave him in the house

or the car while you do this), go into a place with a corner. This could be the corner of a field, or a right angle between your garden walls, or where two fences meet. Hide a dummy in this corner. Now go and get puppy. Take him to one edge of the corner, about ten or fifteen feet in a straight line from where you have hidden the dummy and send him out to fetch. If all has gone well with your previous exercises, your pup will go off in a straight line down the field edge just as in his earlier exercises, and guess what, he will find a retrieve. As he gets better at the exercise you can send him from different places and longer distances. Always hide the dummy in the corner though. The idea of this is to make it easier for the puppy because everywhere leads into the corner, so he's much less likely to over-run the dummy or not find it.

6. *Distractions* – When puppy is coming back with a retrieve, especially when you are using your path, roll a tennis ball past his nose. This is a big temptation for a pup and most will break and go to get it. Just tell pup to 'leave' and then blow your 'come' whistle. Puppy should immediately abandon the chase of the tennis ball and come back to you. Hopefully he will still be carrying the dummy, but if he has dropped it, just sit him up and go and get it yourself at the same time as getting the tennis ball. Do keep practising the occasional 'distraction' as it is very useful to be able to control your dog in that kind of situation when it happens in day-to-day life.

7. *Chosen retrieves* – This exercise is really a bit of a party piece, and usually specifically used for gundog working trials or obedience competitions. But it is worth learning all the same because it shows that you have your dog absolutely concentrating on doing exactly what you are asking, rather than what he is expecting to ask, or just a version of what he wants to do. Sit your dog up about ten metres in front of a fence or wall that is running from side to side in front of you. Throw a dummy so that it lands near the wall and well to the right of you and the dog. Naturally your obedient pup will stay still. Next throw another dummy near the wall, well to the left of you and pup. You now ask your puppy to go and fetch the first dummy. For a dog it is a natural instinct to go and fetch the last object he saw fall, so you are going against the grain. Use your body language to shield the most recent dummy from

the dog and point him in the direction of the first dummy. He should get the message. Having got the first dummy, he's likely to want to go straight to the second dummy and get that at the same time, so again, get your body between him and the second dummy (you may have to sprint a bit). Take the first dummy from him and walk him back to where you started before sending him to fetch the second dummy. Mix up which dummies you retrieve, and sometimes fetch one or even both yourself. This way your pup is on his toes all the time and knows he must listen carefully to what you want.

Warning: retrieving sticks – please don't throw sticks for your dog; there are a huge number of accidents every year where dogs enthusiastically chasing and retrieving sticks have spiked themselves on the stick, which can lead to very dangerous puncture wounds.

▶ *An old soft dummy is easier for a youngster*

Leaving items

Right from the very first retrieving lesson, puppy learns the meaning of the instruction 'leave'. The main point of this is to teach him to be obedient and steady and wait before rushing into fetch something. It originates from gundog training, where it is very important for the dog to be totally under control the whole time because he is working among live animals. However, I have found that I use the instruction 'leave' for all sorts of reasons, and that it is just as useful in the park as in the field. There are so many things around that you really don't want your pup to pick up, that it is really useful to be able to tell him 'leave' and know that you are not going to have to deal with whatever the horrid item might be. Or if he's about to make a bid for someone's picnic sausage, the same applies.

Heeling

Personally, this is the aspect of puppy training which I find hardest to achieve well. Partly this is because the kind of breeds I work with tend to be very active and find trotting along beside me particularly boring, so it can be a stressful activity for all concerned. The best way to start is by having your pup on the lead, and establishing that he is walking comfortably alongside you, at your pace, rather than tugging or hanging back. Now use the verbal instruction 'heel' and the visual signal of slapping your thigh on the side you want him to heel. Walk forward about ten paces before turning sharp right, then walking another few paces before turning left. Then randomly continue walking around the place, sometimes turning back on yourself completely or walking in a circle. This is more interesting for the pup than walking in a straight line and makes him concentrate on you more and stay beside you because he doesn't know what you are going to do next. After a couple of short lessons practising this, the next time you do it, continue as normal but just let go of the lead halfway through the lesson and let it drag along the ground. Hopefully pup will not notice you have done this, but if he does and tries to take advantage of it, it is easy just to tread on the lead and bring him up short. Once you have him trotting alongside you with the lead dragging, the next stage is to unclip it from his collar, so now he is free, but the idea is that he will still continue in the habit of heeling alongside you, even though he is now officially off the lead.

I'm afraid I have found that a lot of pups work this ploy out immediately, and call your bluff! One of the best solutions I have come up with for this is to have one of his favourite toys in my hand. I can wave this about a bit and tease him a little with it just to kid him along and keep him interested in being by my leg. Occasionally I give him the toy as a reward for heeling. This is one of the occasions where you could also use a food treat, held in your hand, as an encouragement and reward. Keep slapping your thigh from time to time to keep him interested. Remember to change direction all the time in order to keep him guessing. If you are lucky enough to have a very narrow green lane

▶ *Ready to start an exercise heeling on the lead*

or alley near where you live, this can also be a good place for training heelwork. The lane will be too narrow for the pup to go anywhere except alongside your leg, and if he does try to make a dash ahead, it is simple for you to reach down and put your hand in front of his nose to let him know he can't go forward.

It is easy to forget that heeling is part of obedience for your dog, and that it is something he has to make an effort to do, just as much as any of the other exercises we teach him. A lot of people have their pups on heel, and then forget about it, leaving the young pup having to concentrate quite hard for a long period of time while the boss is just wandering along enjoying a country walk or chatting to friends. If you are not going to do anything else with your pup for a while, put him back on the lead so that he can relax and know he doesn't have to think about anything.

◀ *Tread on the trailing lead to get the dog to pay attention when teaching heeling*

Release

At the beginning of life, as a young puppy, most of your pup's learning was done through play, and running around developed seamlessly into running with a purpose. Now though, as your young dog becomes more highly trained, and his lessons more demanding, it is time to make more of a difference between 'school work' and 'playtime'. You should introduce some kind of release instruction to let your pup know that now is his moment to have a bit of an unstructured run around. I usually use the phrase 'go play' or 'playtime' as it sounds very different from any of the other serious commands. At the end of a lesson, or at the end of a particular exercise if you want pup to have a bit of a break, give him his release phrase so he knows he can stop concentrating for a while. Make sure you are in a safe place for pup to run free before you let him go.

TRAINING BY THE PLACEBOARD METHOD
with Ian and Wendy Openshaw

What are placeboards?

A placeboard is a low, square platform about six inches high and eighteen inches square, covered in artificial turf (for the dog's comfort). Generally four are laid out in a square for training. The main exercise is teaching the pup to sit calmly on the board, and then learning a series of lessons, each of which ends up with the pup sitting quietly on the board ready to be praised and rewarded. You can make the boards yourself out of plywood but it's probably easier just to check out Ian and Wendy's website: rytexgundogs.com

Why are they becoming a popular method of training?

Ian first came across placeboards when he was judging working dog competitions in America and was impressed with how easy young pups found it to learn lessons when they were working using placeboards. For those with shortages of time and space – particularly if you are trying to train your pup in an urban area – the placeboards are very helpful. They need very little space, you can even set them up in a garage. It's also quick and easy to set up a range of training situations using the boards.

Why do they work?

The short answer to this question is that nobody really knows! Ian explains: 'All the time when you are training a pup, you want to make it as easy as possible for him to get it right. With the placeboards everything is very straightforward for the pup. He knows exactly where he is meant to sit – that is, on the board – and when he is sitting on the board he is confident he is doing the right thing. Each exercise finishes with the pup sitting on the board being praised, so it is a very good training structure.'

Wendy adds: 'I think the board is a bit of a comfort blanket for a young pup. If you think of it, they are quite like a little dog bed, and I think it is a bit of a secure place for them. If they are ever getting confused by an exercise, they can just come and sit on the board for a moment and get themselves together. It helps keep everything very calm, controlled and predictable.'

How can I use them?

If you are short of time and space, the simplest way to use placeboards is to lay two or three out in your garage or anywhere that is big enough to get about three metres between each board. Then you can do all the various coming, sitting, staying, stopping and retrieving lessons outlined above. The only difference is that the start and finish of each exercise is on one of the placeboards. You can also add in the instruction: 'place' to tell the pup to sit on the board. If you have a bit more time and space, try the placeboard lesson illustrated here.

A placeboard lesson with step-by-step illustrations

◀ *Placeboards can be used for any breed of dog, even Cathy, the bull terrier cross*

One: Sit pup on placeboard and add the verbal instruction, 'place'. Use of the lead is optional, depending what stage your pup is at.

Two: Make sure the pup is sitting attentively on the board and then walk over to the next board and call your pup with voice and hand signal.

Three: Next, send the pup away from where you both are on the placeboard and onto the next one. You can walk a stride or two with him until he gets the idea. Remember to use the instruction 'place'.

Four: Soon you will be able to send pup from one placeboard to another while you stay where you are. Now you can start introducing all sorts of variations, including retrieves. For more details, visit rytexgundogs.com

Here is a simple check list that puppy is learning all his different exercises. If you are confident he is achieving this key stage, then put him through the Puppy Graduation Test at the end of this section.

- Puppy always comes immediately when called by voice, whistle and hand signal
- Puppy sits when asked by voice, whistle and hand signal and remains sitting
- Puppy stops instantly when asked by voice, whistle and hand signal at distances up to fifty metres
- Puppy enjoys retrieving items and happily brings them back to you
- Puppy remains calm and under control when he is playing retrieving games
- Puppy will leave an item and not pick it up if instructed to leave it
- Puppy walks to heel whether on or off the lead
- Puppy remains obedient even when there are exciting distractions
- Puppy is happy and boisterous, yet quickly obedient when asked to be

Frequently Asked Questions about six months onwards

Q. Our puppy is just a family pet, we don't want to do competitions, so why should we bother with all this training?

A. There's no need to bother with it, but of course then you will have to bother to try to catch your dog when he's run off and won't come back; or bother to apologise when he's knocked over a pushchair; or bother to clear up when he's trashed the house. And while you are doing all that, what you won't be doing is feeling the warm glow of pride when someone admires your dog; or the reassuring pleasure of your pup gazing up at you adoringly. Your relationship with your pup is like so many relationships in life – you can put in a little extra now and get a lot back down the line.

Q. How long should each training session be?

A. At the very beginning of his training, your pup won't even know he is having a lesson. Instead training is just 'playing with a purpose'. Five or ten minutes is plenty. Be alert to signs that your pup is tiring or losing interest. Later on, as he is learning more complex instructions, the length of training sessions will extend, but I try not to go on for more than twenty minutes. It is easy for you and pup to get so absorbed with what you are doing that you can go on too long.

Q. How often should I do training sessions?

A. Whenever you are interacting or playing with your puppy he is learning from you. It is more important to make sure every interaction is positive and helpful, than to be rigid in scheduling 'lessons'. While I was planning this book, Fizz was a very tiny puppy mainly living on the lawn in front of my office window, and I used to pop out and spend five minutes with her every time I had a screen break from my computer. Later on, we were having more formal lessons, and I would do two or sometimes three short training sessions each day. For training to work well, you do need to be able to spend some proper time with your puppy every day. Saving training for weekends and not interacting much with pup the rest of the week slows training down and makes it much less natural and instinctive for the pup to learn.

Q. Why is it that my puppy obeys when close, but not when further away?

A. Surprisingly, this is actually a sign that he isn't really obeying you when close! It may seem as if your puppy is responding correctly to your instructions, but if you check carefully what you are doing, you may well notice that it takes you a couple of repeats of a command before pup obeys, and your lessons all round may have got a bit imprecise or lazy. Go through the various exercises in this chapter, and especially repeat the checks in Key Stage Three. Now be honest with yourself; how well did puppy really do? Take your training back a step or two and this time insist that everything is done 100 per cent. Once you have this, you can gradually increase the distance work.

Q. Puppy won't bring the ball back, what should I do?

A. Far from all dogs are natural retrievers, and some breeds enjoy retrieving more than others. If your pup doesn't really take to it, then that might not be an activity to continue with. If he does seem to enjoy retrieving, but the penny hasn't dropped about actually bringing the item back, then just go back to an earlier stage of training. When he does bring something back, leave it in his mouth for a while before taking it, and give him plenty of praise so he realises this is the right thing to do. When he first picks up the item, you can also remember to blow your 'come' whistle and take a few steps away from pup. He will soon get the message that the game can only go on if he brings the item back.

This test is to give you an objective measure of where your puppy is in his training. Don't use it as training or train for it. Certainly don't worry if it doesn't go smoothly – just backtrack for a while and try again in a couple of weeks. If your pup sails through, then it's off to university in the next section of this book!

1. With puppy playing freely, allow him to get at least fifty metres from you (you can also hide if there is an opportunity). Call him to come by voice, whistle and once he has seen you, by visual signal. He must come immediately, straight to you.

Pass ☐   Fail ☐

2. Sit puppy up and walk away to a distance of twenty to fifty metres. Wander around randomly; chuck some toys; jump up and down; call a name that is nothing like pup's name. He should stay sat looking at you.

Pass ☐   Fail ☐

3. Have puppy heeling alongside you, off the lead. Give the whistle signal for stop, but keep walking yourself. Puppy should sit and watch you, even though you haven't stopped.

Pass ☐   Fail ☐

4. As puppy is playing around, blow your stop whistle and give a visual signal, at the same time as throwing a retrieve in the air. Tell pup to 'leave' and walk up to him where he is sat before then sending him to fetch the retrieve. Pup should stop on command and make no attempt to fetch the item until you go up and instruct him to.

Pass ☐   Fail ☐

5. Go to a public place where dogs are allowed off the lead and repeat the tests above. Pup's performance should be identical, no matter what the distractions.

Pass ☐   Fail ☐

6. Arrange to have to some friends over that pup doesn't know well.

Get into situations where you are chatting with them (or people you may happen to meet when out and about). Instruct pup to sit/stay while you are talking. He should remain obedient, even if there is another dog.

Pass ☐   Fail ☐

All passes? Congratulations! You have trained your young dog all the way from puppy to perfect! At this point you have a young dog to be proud of for the rest of his life, even if you do nothing else at all. If you are both enjoying training, there is a whole world of canine activity out there that your young dog is now very well prepared to join in with. For example, he would be equipped to perform novice obedience work now, with almost no further training. You could also try working tests. Check out Part Five for all the different 'canine universities' available!

PART FOUR: SUMMARY

'BIG SCHOOL' TRAINING FROM ABOUT SIX MONTHS

Here's a quick reminder of the things covered in this section.

In this part of the book, you and your pup have finally put it all together to take your training as far as you will need to have the perfect family dog. You've learnt how to develop those early commands into a full vocabulary so that your young dog will now come, sit, stay, heel and retrieve exactly as you instruct him, whether with voice, whistle or hand signals. Your perfect youngster loves to please you, and always cooperates with what you ask, no matter what distractions there might be. This is a young dog you can be proud of for the rest of your lives together.

PART FIVE

YOUR BEST FRIEND

As you and your young dog near the end of your first year together, now it is time to have some real fun! If you have been doing it right, all of you – puppy, family, you, even friends and neighbours – will have been thoroughly enjoying the months of basic training. They are really the equivalent of secondary school for pups. By now though, he will have passed loads of doggy GCSEs and maybe his canine A-levels. He will be doing all you would wish for in a pleasant companion dog – coming to call, sitting, staying, heeling, fetching, following your hand signals, even performing all sorts of little tasks and tricks. Now it is time to think of university.

▶ *Diving into icy water*

There is a whole world of activity out there for an intelligent, educated young dog and his human. This section of the book gives you a brief introduction, and who to contact, for all the different hobbies and competitions you and your dog can take part in (full website details etc. for each activity are given at the back of the book). You don't have to do any of them, but I do recommend giving one or two a try. I stumbled into gundog work completely by chance, and I have met the best bunch of people and dogs and made lifelong friends through it.

▶ *By the time your pup is a perfect young dog, he will do anything for you: fetch a dummy*

▲ *… dive into icy water*

◀ *… and gaze adoringly at you*

Kennel Club activities

Many people think of the Kennel Club as being all about posh dogs trotting round the show ring at Crufts, but that is only a tiny part of what the Kennel Club does here in the UK, and it is a similar situation with the American Kennel Club. The Kennel Club is really all about enhancing the shared lives of dogs and humans. Their charitable trust does a huge amount of work behind the scenes, and it is well worth looking at that section on the club's website (see back of the book for details). Another big element of the Kennel Club's work is organising dog-related activities for all ages. Here is a selection.

The Good Citizen Dog Scheme – The largest dog training programme in the UK and open to all dogs, young or old, pedigree or crossbreed, whether Kennel Club registered or not. You can join one of about 1,800 dog training clubs around the country which run the scheme, and train your dog to earn certificates of achievement. Your dog doesn't have to be super-fit or brilliant to take part; the scheme is non-competitive and

▼ *If you have a pedigree dog, showing is an option*

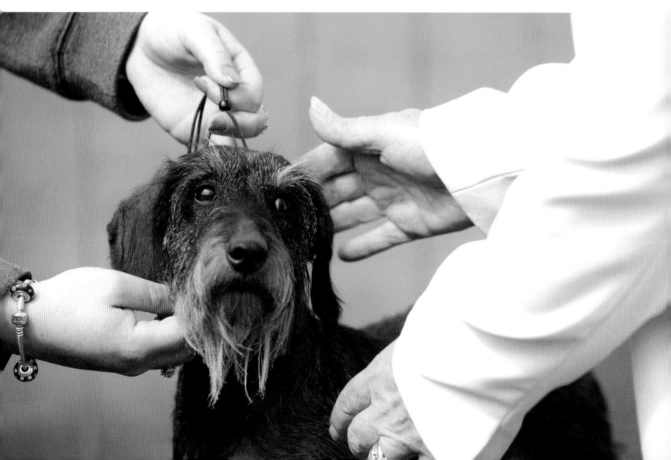

emphasis is placed on the dog reaching its potential. There are four levels of courses from Puppy Foundation, to Bronze, Silver, and Gold Awards. More info at the Kennel Club website or your vet.

The Young Kennel Club – Ideal if one of the children has really got into training and looking after your puppy, the club is designed to help children learn new skills, build confidence and make new friends through dog training. It starts from age six right though to twenty-six years old, and has a massive year round diary of events countrywide. More info at the Kennel Club website.

Pedigree dog showing – Of course, the Kennel Club runs Crufts Dog Show, the most famous dog show in the world, each spring at the Birmingham NEC. Crufts however, is just the tip of an iceberg of dog shows running all year round throughout the country. They are run by the different pedigree breed societies, under the supervision of the Kennel Club. If you have a pedigree pup you are particularly proud of then you might think about showing. Go along to Crufts and see what you think.

▼ *Careful preparation is needed for the show ring*

Companion Dog Club and shows – You don't have to have a pedigree pooch to have a bit of fun. The Kennel Club organises a series of informal charity dog shows all over the country which any dog can enter. There is also a special **Companion Dog Club** to make your dog feel special even if he's just a mongrel mutt, and it's a great way for the family and the dog to have a bit of fun together. You can even take part in a version of Crufts for ordinary dogs, called Scruffts, and the final of the competition is held at Crufts each year. For more information go to the Kennel Club website.

Obedience training and competition

If the training you have done so far with this book has gone well and your pup has taken to it easily, you may not realise it, but you are already well on the way to having a dog that is obedient enough to compete at obedience classes. You have probably seen these televised and marvelled at the amazingly close bond between the dog and his owner, usually referred to as the 'handler'. But think about it – if you and your pup have already progressed happily through this book, the bond between the two of you is likely to be just as good as anything you may see on the telly! All you need is a little bit of formal polishing up and you too could be the admiration of everyone at Crufts!

Formal obedience training and competitions are overseen by the Kennel Club, so you can visit the website to find the details of a club near you. If you decide to enter a competition, there are six levels: Pre-Beginners and Beginners Classes are for first-timers; then the classes gradually become more demanding up to level C. Each class contains a set of exercises which the judge will ask you and your dog to perform. These range from heelwork (on and off the lead), to a recall, control exercises such as a one-minute sit and a two-minute down stay, becoming progressively more difficult as you go to each new level. When you reach Class C your dog will have to perform additional exercises such as a scent discrimination exercise and also a send away and distant control exercise.

Each exercise is given a maximum number of points and judges will judge each team (handler and dog) against their personal view of the perfect execution of the test (under the guidance set within the regulations). Dogs are expected to work in a happy and natural manner, with the handler responding smartly and quickly to the commands dictated out loud by the 'caller steward'.

Heelwork to Music

Another of the 'arena disciplines' where the dogs are working and competing mainly indoors or in the show ring or arena, is Heelwork to Music, which has become a competitive event only fairly recently as a development from the heelwork element of obedience competition. Some viewers describe Heelwork to Music as 'dressage for dogs'. The 'Best in Show' evening at Crufts usually features a demonstration of HTM, where the dog and handler together perform a dance-based stage routine to music. In competition, participants devise routines of up to four minutes, set to music, and perform the routines with their dog. HTM is divided into two categories – Heelwork to Music and Freestyle – and most shows stage official classes in both categories. The introduction of Freestyle – routines interpreting the music in which predefined heelwork movements form only a third or less of the total – has added to the growing appeal of the sport. Heelwork to Music has a wide range of facets, from a creative 'play' environment where pet owners develop a bond with their dogs, to opportunities for more competitive training and competition, to an enthralling and moving spectator event. The Kennel Club oversees the various competitions.

Agility competition

First introduced to the UK at Crufts in 1978, agility competitions have rapidly become one of the most popular of all the dog disciplines, with both competitors and spectators alike. The most famous competitions are held at the Olympia Horse Show just before Christmas and at Crufts in the spring, but there are more than 300 licensed agility shows held annually. Sometimes described as 'showjumping for dogs', the dogs have to whizz over, round and through a number of obstacles including jumps, tunnels, a bridge, weaving poles and sometimes jump through hoops, as well as sitting still for a few seconds in the middle of it all. It makes compulsive viewing as the dogs so obviously enjoy it, rushing round the obstacles with tails wagging furiously and the occasional joyful bark, while their handlers puff along behind trying to keep up. Athletic, intelligent dogs like collies and spaniels excel in this sphere, but there are classes for different sizes of dog. As long as he can jump, your dog will have a chance. Nor does he have to be a pedigree to take part, but he will need to be KC registered either via the Activity Register (for non-pedigrees) or the Breed Register (for pedigrees).

As with most training specialisations, training for agility usually starts when your dog is about a year old, when he will be mature and strong enough for the demands of the sport, and you can't enter a competition until he is at least eighteen months old. The organising body insists that your dog must be fully socialised and that you can control him at

▲ *The collie breeds have natural agility*

all times, especially as your dog will be competing off-lead – now you can see why you bothered to go through all the early training in this book! Joining an Agility Club is a good idea to get training and practice, and you can find your nearest by using the Kennel Club's 'Find a Club' tool on their website.

Flyball

Originating from America, Flyball first appeared in the UK in 1990. If your dog is bold, athletic and fit, he will be ideal for Flyball. Many dogs that just get too overexcited to win agility competitions, take to Flyball instantly. In Flyball two relay teams of dogs compete at the same time, each using a parallel 'racing lane' down which each dog in turn runs, clearing four hurdles in succession before triggering a pedal on the Flyball box. A tennis ball is then released which the dog must hold before returning over the hurdles to the start line. The first team to have its fourth dog across the finish line, with any part of the dog's body, wins the race. Each dog must cross the finish line before the next dog can start, and handlers aim to launch their dog so that he will cross with a returning dog just at the line. The area needed for a Flyball race tends to be fairly large because the dogs can run at terrific speeds and need a good distance at the end of the race to slow down. A wide area at the end of the hurdles gives the dogs enough room to pick up the ball and reverse direction safely. It's traditional for the dogs to leap up into their owners' arms at the end of a successful run, and great fun for the spectators to see people being nearly bowled over in the excitement. It's a wonderful chance to see dogs showing off their athletic skills and drive. Another great advantage of Flyball is that it is a team sport and a tremendous opportunity to bond with other dog owners. In fact a recent Flyball final featured a husband and wife who had met through Flyball – but ended up competing against each other on different teams! The absolute top Flyball dogs are collies, but you often seen spaniels, pointers and crossbreeds competing successfully. Flyball clubs are often run in conjunction with agility work, and you can find your local one online or through the Kennel Club.

Rally

The newest of the dog sports, the big plus point of Rally (known as Rally O in America) is that it incorporates a little bit of several different dog disciplines – a sort of cross between obedience and agility. You and your dog have to complete a course which includes a number of different exercises. Some are the sort of obstacles you might meet in agility, like a jump or weaving in a serpentine; others are the kind of thing you are expected to do in obedience, like a controlled sit, heelwork and sending away. The atmosphere is very relaxed, and at the introductory levels dogs compete on a loose lead. It is only at the more advanced stages that you will need precise heeling.

The exercises are selected and course designed by the judge on the day. Each individual round is performed at a 'brisk pace' and takes about four minutes. There is no direction from the judge or steward as in obedience, instead signs tell the competitor which exercise to perform. Handlers walk through the course (without dogs) before the competition starts. The handler may give verbal commands and encouragement throughout as necessary. Competitors start each round with a perfect score of 200 and deductions are made by the judge for inaccuracies and mistakes in performance. Rally is a good way to get into working with your dog, and there is plenty of information available through the Kennel Club.

Working Trials

Working Trials date back to 1924 when the Associated Sheep, Police and Army Dog Society (ASPADS) held the first event. Originally based on training for police work, nowadays the working trials are purely sporting and are run outdoors, year round. Working Trials tests are broken down into three main sections:

1. *Nosework*
Nosework comprises search and track exercises. The dog follows a track laid by a 'tracklayer' (who is a stranger to the dog) walking a set pattern

designed by the judge and identical for each dog. The track is approximately half a mile long and laid on grassland, arable fields or heathland, with each competitor working on similar terrain to others in the stake. As the dog follows the track it has to seek out and recover articles placed along the track by the tracklayer. The track is laid at different times, before the dog work begins, depending on the level of the competition. The other component of nosework is 'search' where the dog has to search for and retrieve articles placed in a marked area.

2. *Agility*

To test his agility, the dog must clear three obstacles – a three-foot hurdle, a six-foot-high wooden scale and a nine-foot-long jump. Two attempts may be permitted for each obstacle.

3. *Control*

There are various exercises in this section. **Heelwork** – the dog must walk with his shoulder reasonably close to the handler while the handler navigates their way around people and obstacles at different speeds. **Sendaway** – involves sending the dog away across a minimum distance of fifty yards, the handler will then redirect the dog through a series of commands. **Retrieving a dumbbell** – the dog must retrieve a dumbbell which has been thrown by the handler. **Down stay** – the dog must stay in the down position while the handler is out of sight for a period of time. **Steadiness to gunshot** – the dog is tested on his reactions to gunshot. The dog will be penalised if he shows any signs of fear or aggression. **Speak** – the dog is ordered to 'speak' and cease 'speaking' on command by the handler with a minimum of commands and/or signals.

Almost any dog of any breed can take part in Working Trials, provided they are fit and healthy, but the shepherd dogs – German and Belgian Shepherds and Alsatians – always do well, as do Rottweilers and other breeds traditionally associated with police work. Any Kennel Club registered dogs (pedigree or non-pedigree) can take part, but they must be eighteen months old before they can compete at a Working Trial.

As with most dog disciplines, there are clubs countrywide for training and holding competitions. With Trials being quite a complex competition, events and training often take place over a few days, so

▲ *A range of activities combines retrieves with obedience*

the social scene on the human side is just as much fun as the competition is for the dogs. Combining so many different elements of all round training including obedience, agility, gundog scenting work, etc. training for Working Trials is quite a commitment – but if you have already sailed through the exercises in this book you have every chance of success. Before you get started it's a good idea to go along to a Trial and find out what's involved.

Hound work

Bloodhound Trials

Bloodhounds are distinguished from other breeds by their extraordinary olfactory powers, which enable them to hunt entirely by airborne scent. They are the oldest breed of sporting dogs which hunt by scent, and Bloodhound Trials enable the hounds to demonstrate the remarkable abilities for which they have been bred – a fine illustration of dogs that are 'Fit For Function: Fit For Life'. Bloodhound Working Trials are open to purebred bloodhounds only. The trials are a challenging and exciting countryside activity in which hounds follow a human scent trail over a 'line' up to three miles long. The line has been laid by a 'runner' up to two hours previously, following a pre-determined route set by the judge and marked on a map. When 'hunting the clean boot', as it is termed, the hound must follow the scent, ignoring all distractions, and at the end of the line he must go up to and positively identify the runner, who will be standing in a line-up with two other participants. Identification usually takes the form of two large (muddy) paws placed on the runner's chest!

Hound Trailing

The original home of this ancient sport, which dates back to the eighteenth century, is Britain's Lake District, where it is still very popular, with Hound Trailing meetings held twelve times a week throughout Cumbria during the season, which lasts from April until October. The Hound Trailing Association of the UK was formed under the direction of Robert Jefferson in 1906. Racing takes place over moorland, fields and fells, the hounds following a trail made of a mixture of paraffin and oil of aniseed. Two trailers carry rags to the halfway point and then walk away from each other, one towards the start and one towards the finish, laying the trail. As the race unfolds many of the owners and spectators lay bets with the bookmakers who are a permanent part of the trailing fraternity. When the timekeeper shouts 'trail', the race is close to finishing, and the betting stops. The first dog to cross the line wins. Judging the result of a Hound Trail can often be a close call, with a video camera 'photo finish' sometimes used to decide the result. If you are holidaying in the Lake District you may

▼ *Greyhounds use their speed in competition*

suddenly come across a field full of cars, with men and women standing with binoculars in hand, a line of people will be shouting and cheering, calling out names and blowing whistles – and if you are a hound owner, preferably a foxhound, then there is a great temptation to get involved with the sport. For more information, visit www.houndtrailing.org.uk.

Lure-coursing

This sport, just as ancient as Hound Trailing, also uses a lure for the hounds to chase. But with lure-coursing, the hounds used are 'sight' or 'gaze' hounds. So instead of using their noses to follow a scent trail along the ground, the hounds use their eyes to chase or course the lure by sight. The course is laid out before the trial, generally in a fenced field. The course is approximately 500 yards long and usually includes some straight runs and a number of turns. The field is checked for anything that could be a danger to the hounds (holes, for example). During the event dogs follow an artificial lure around a course on an open field. Coursing dogs are scored on speed, enthusiasm, agility, endurance, and their ability to follow the lure.

When the course is called, hounds line up in the collecting ring to be organised into pairs to go out to the Huntmaster and the starting line. The Huntmaster gives the signal to release the hounds with a 'Tally Ho!' In the UK most lure-coursing is run by the British Sighthound Field Association (www.lurecousing.org.uk) and in America the sport is run by the American Sighthound Field Association (www.asfa.org.uk). Both organisations are keen for anyone with a sighthound – which includes anything from the traditional greyhound to Afghans and salukis – to have a go. They stress: your hound will probably love it. Even the most pampered and dignified of sighthounds can rarely resist the opportunity to chase and catch something – anything! It's a great way to keep your hound healthy and physically and mentally fit. A hound in proper shape is trim and muscular, with heart, lungs and circulation in peak condition. It gives you a chance to evaluate your hound in a way the show ring cannot. Sighthounds are beautiful, but they are functional animals too. A judge in the ring can certainly evaluate beauty, type and the potential to function adequately in the field. But these judges do not see the hounds run, turn, recover from a fall, so cannot evaluate speed, agility, determination, courage – the qualities so important in a coursing hound. Lure-coursing demands and values all these qualities.

The best hound for coursing is usually the greyhound, but others that are successful include the Afghan (a wonderful sight at full gallop); the deer- and wolfhounds; the borzoi (or Russian wolfhound); whippets; the saluki; the basenji; the borzaya; and the Pharaoh (although there is some dispute over whether this is genuinely a sighthound).

▼ *For sighthound breeds, lure-coursing is great fun*

The Great British Greyhound Walk

One of the newest of all the canine activities, The Great British Greyhound Walk began in 2010 when a group of greyhound and lurcher owners who walk most weekends in Essex, Suffolk, Norfolk and Hertfordshire came together to walk their dogs as a special occasion. Since then the event has become international, with walks throughout Europe, Australia, New Zealand, Canada and America. Every year, large group-walks are held nationwide on the same day, as one huge family, promoting greyhounds one step at a time and bringing together many other sighthounds, to raise awareness and show members of the public just what wonderful pets greyhounds make. In 2014, nearly 3,5000 greyhounds and other sighthounds were walked on the same day, with more than 500 more joining in worldwide. Smaller walks are held by local greyhound groups throughout the year. A spin-off from the walk has been a competition for customised bandanas worn by the dogs, which was won in 2014 by a First World War Centenary bandana. The greyhound walkers are having great fun with their dogs, and to join in, just visit www.greatbritishgreyhoundwalk.org.uk.

Canicross

Rather faster than greyhound walking, canicross is the sport of running off-road with your dog. The human participant wears a waistbelt which attaches via a two metre bungee line to a padded dog harness. It is a fantastic way to keep you and your dog fit whilst enjoying the great outdoors together. It provides a physical workout for your dog and the use of directional commands will help him to learn to use his brain and build up his confidence.

There are various different groups offering canicross activities, with one of the most popular being the Trailrunners (www.canicross.org.uk). This organisation welcomes adults and children, both novice and experienced, who want to get fit with their dog in a friendly and supportive environment. People are able to start canimarching (walking) and can progress to canicross (running) at their own pace.

Beginners can join a local club and meet up with a canicrosser for a walk, run and introduction to the sport. More experienced participants have the chance to compete in cross-country trials. The organisation has adapted a number of outdoor sports like hash running, canyoneering and canoeing to include dogs. So you can take part in 'canihashing', 'caniteering' and 'caniobility' among others.

Dogs need to be a year old before they are physically mature enough to start taking part, and eighteen months old before they can compete seriously. In the beginning the sled-dog type breeds like huskies were mainly used, but nowadays people use all sorts of dogs including gundogs, hounds, collies, and even some smaller dogs. A certain amount of training is necessary at the beginning, and it's best to do this with the help of an experienced canicrosser, as the harness can be a bit difficult to manage. Some breeds of dog, like spaniels, do not run in straight lines and have to learn how to do this; while many of the hound breeds have a tendency to take off unpredictably. And, of course, physical fitness for both dog and human is important!

Sled-dogging and bikejor

Surprisingly, this sport is thriving in the UK since, contrary to what you might expect, it doesn't actually require any snow! Off Snow, or Dryland as it is more commonly known, is one of the fastest growing dog sports in the northern hemisphere. Instead of pulling a sled, the team of dogs (or pairs or individuals depending on the discipline) is hitched to a specially adapted vehicle so they can dash off over dry land just as easily as they would over snow. The big teams of eight or so dogs can easily pull any multi-terrain vehicle, and there are now many venues over the UK where you can just go along for the ride without even having a dog. Of course, if it actually snows as well, the whole experience is magical.

Britain has been leading the way in this sport in the European arena for some time, but worldwide, teams from Canada and America dominate. The UK sled dog racing season holds around sixty competitive sled dog races across the country by around ten different sled-dog clubs or organisations.

Approximately 300–400 teams race on a regular basis in the UK running a variety of breeds from Siberian huskies to Scandinavian hounds, Alaskan malamutes to Alaskan huskies, Samoyeds, Greenland and Canadian Eskimo dogs. However, don't be put off if your dog isn't one of the traditional breeds. Many of the most successful sledders like to have at least one or two German pointers on the team to add reliability.

Dog drivers, or mushers as they are known, compete using high performance wheeled 'rigs' designed especially for the sport. The UK is a world leader in rig manufacture with several different makes being sold to mushers inside and outside the UK. Team sizes can range in size from one-dog canicross, scooter and bikejor teams to eight-dog sled teams.

Bikejor is popular across Europe, and is similar to skijor. In skijor, dogs or even horses are used to pull skiers, and there is a famous race in Wyoming, USA annually. Bikejor can be enjoyed all year round, and uses one or two dogs to pull a tricycle-style rig, with a frame for the driver – a bit like a modern chariot! There are lots of different clubs to join, depending on what breed of dog you have, and the umbrella organisation in the UK is the British Sleddog Sports Federation at www.sleddogsports.gb.com.

Gundog work

Gundog breeds like Labrador retrievers, spaniels and setters are the most popular of all the breeds, not just in Britain but also in America and Europe, so it's not surprising that there are many activities and competitions that are designed just for them, as well as being able to take part in all the other general dog activities. The specialist gundog activities are called Field Trials and Working Tests. Field Trials have a long history, and originated as a way to find the very best dogs to create breeding lines. Today their function is very similar, as they are there to test that no faults in working ability, temperament or health have crept into the breed. The gundog's original function, as the name suggests, was to work closely with his human handler when he was out shooting game birds like pheasant, grouse and partridge as well as rabbits. The dogs are used to find where the game is; to flush it so that the shooter can shoot it safely; and then to retrieve the dead game or find any game that might have run away wounded. Even today, every keen Shot considers it vital to have a dog working alongside to perform this function. Without a good dog it is possible that wounded game might

▼ *Gundog work is an enjoyable activity*

be lost, and it is also very difficult to manoeuvre the game in such a way that it can be shot safely. A Field Trial is carried out in a very similar way to a normal shooting outing, with live game being shot and retrieved during the trial. After the trial, the game is sold to local restaurants and farm shops.

A Working Test is different, because no live game is used and there is no shooting other than the occasional firing of a starting pistol or small

▼ *You don't have to shoot to take part in Field Trials*

gun to simulate a gunshot. In Working Tests canvas dummies of various sizes are used instead of live game. These are thrown into positions or hidden, to simulate the kind of tasks a gundog might face on a shooting day. It doesn't test your dog's ability to find live game, but it does challenge him to find retrieves in all manner of different places, including in lakes and across streams. He also has to show that he is obedient and steady to your commands – not a problem for your young dog if he has been managing everything in the book so far!

The good news is that you don't have to shoot to get involved in gundog sports – in fact you will be even more welcome if you don't want to shoot! Most of the people involved in shooting sports want to be able to do the shooting and not bother with the vital gundog work. So people who are prepared to do the gundog work without demanding their turn to have a go at the shooting are very much in demand! Nor do you have to compete. All over the country – probably right on your doorstep without you even knowing it – there are shoots going on. These shoots are always in need of help from people with well-trained dogs. The best way to find out more about all this is to join your local gundog club. There are hundreds of them throughout the country, even in London, and their details are listed on the Kennel Club website.

Sheep dog trialling

In 1873 the first recorded sheep dog trials were held in Bala, North Wales, but it was not until some thirty-three years later that The International Sheep Dog Society (ISDS) was formed, following a meeting of English and Scottish sheepmen in 1906. Shortly afterwards the first International Trials were held in Gullane, Scotland and, except during the war years, have continued to be an annual event. Now over one hundred years later, the ISDS has well over 6,000 members from all over the world. If your dog is an ISDS-registered border collie, have a think about shepherding work, training and trialling. There are dozens of clubs countrywide to give you an introduction. Have a look at the various contact details at the back of the book to find something near you.

Search and rescue

Becoming a search and rescue dog handler isn't a competitive sport, but it is probably the most difficult and rewarding thing you can do with your dog. Armed and emergency forces worldwide have their own trained dogs to perform search and rescue tasks, particularly in disasters and emergencies. For example, the Greater Manchester Fire Brigade in the UK is well known for its search dogs, and one, Echo, even went out to Haiti to help search for survivors of the earthquake.

In addition, there are a number of civilian dogs and their handlers who volunteer to provide back-up, and to work in cases where it may not be necessary to have an emergency force involved. Typical work would involve assisting mountain rescue workers looking for lost climbers, or in suburban areas the dogs are often used to help search for missing children or vulnerable people.

In Britain there is an umbrella organisation, the National Search and Rescue Dog Association (www.nsarda.co.uk) which brings together the various regional organisations. In the United States there are several different groups, mainly based in the different states, including the American Rescue Dog Association (www.ardainc.org). To get involved with search and rescue work, you will have to start without your dog! Volunteers to be 'bodies' are vital for the specific training of the dogs, and this is what you will do when you first join a search and rescue group. You might find yourself waiting in a snowhole on Cairn Gorm, or lying in a muddy ditch in Somerset, but in the end you will guarantee to be licked by the lovely dog who finds you.

Once you know a bit more about what is required you can start to get your dog involved. If he's a working breed and has already proved himself in his obedience and hopefully done working trials or other scent-based work, there is a good chance your dog will be able to learn the extra skills required to be a fully-fledged search and rescue dog. It generally takes about two years to train, and once trained, the work is often difficult – both physically and emotionally. This is a chance for your dog (and you) to 'do your bit' in real-life dramas, so it's well worth checking out the website of NSARDA (www.nsarda.co.uk).

PART FIVE: SUMMARY

YOUR BEST FRIEND

By the time your pup has grown up to be a young dog of around a year to eighteen months old he will be a credit to you and your work in basic training. Many dogs and their owners don't take the training any further than that, preferring to enjoy their dog purely as a companion and pet. But all over the UK and worldwide, dog owners have discovered a huge number of different activities to be enjoyed alongside their dogs – some of them competitive, and some genuinely life-saving. This section of the book has given a general introduction to those activities. If you like the sound of one or another, you will need to join an organisation and give your dog some additional specialist training. Full details on where to go to get started are at the back of the book.

▲ *Fudge and her granddaughter, Fizz*

Now is the time for you and your dog to enjoy the rest of his life!

▼ *Field Trial Champion Gournaycourt Morag, 'Fudge', has now retired to take up a new role as writer's companion*

Dogs and the law

Of course we all believe our dogs behave faultlessly, and if the training in this book has been going well, your puppy should by now be well on his way to being perfect! Not all dogs behave well though, and badly handled dogs can be a dangerous problem for everyone. It is surprising to discover that there are at least a dozen separate pieces of government legislation relating to dogs. There are times when it is possible for you and your dog to break the law by mistake, and sometimes interfering people will accuse you of breaking the law with your dog even if you haven't. There may also be occasions when you come across a dog owner who is breaking the law in a dangerous way and something needs to be done about it. So for all these reasons it is useful just to have background knowledge of the law on dogs, and hopefully you will never need it.

Caring for dogs

Not everybody is as devoted to their dogs as we are, and to deal with problems of neglect or cruelty to dogs, there is **The Animal Welfare Act 2006.** This says that dogs must not be mutilated, forced to fight or given away as prizes. It also describes an official duty of care for dog owners to provide their animals with suitable housing; proper food; freedom to behave normally; and protection from pain, suffering and disease. Remember, there are many different versions of doggy lifestyles that are suitable and healthy, from the farmyard dog all the way to the pampered pooch. However, if you believe a dog is genuinely suffering, there are several animal welfare organisations which will pursue the problem for you, and you can find details in the contacts section.

Controlling dogs among people

The cases of dogs attacking children and adults have increased over the past couple of decades, and the fashion for keeping 'hard' or even genuinely dangerous dogs is persisting. As a result there are now important laws about this problem, with serious penalties. In 2014 the

Anti-Social Behaviour, Crime and Policing Act added amendments to the existing **Dangerous Dogs Act of 1991** to extend it to cover dangerous incidents on private property and to increase sentences for owners of dangerous dogs, as well as making injuries to assistance dogs an aggravated offence. The existing laws (including the original **Dogs Act of 1871**) already made it a criminal offence for the owner or handler of a dog to be 'dangerously out of control' in a public place. The phrase 'dangerously out of control' means that a dog has already actually injured someone or certainly looks as if he is about to. If a dog actually does injure someone he may be seized by the police, and the penalty can include a prison sentence and a ban on keeping animals as well as a fine and possible compensation payments. This is a really serious offence, so it is important to be aware of it. You may need to know about it if you come under attack, perhaps while out walking your own dog. Bear in mind also that it is possible that if your dog starts chasing, barking and jumping up at small children too vigorously, parents may get frightened or worried enough to make a complaint about you under the Act. This is a very good reason for training our puppies to be perfect!

Controlling dogs among animals

The other really big issue of controlling dogs when they are out and about has been recognised for a long time, which is the problem that dogs instinctively want to chase other animals, especially farm animals. The main law about this, the **Dogs (Protection of Livestock) Act**, actually dates right back to 1953, and if anything the problem has got worse now that people are rambling with their dogs in the countryside so much more. The Act states that no dog must be allowed to chase or attack (known as worrying) any form of livestock on farmland. This doesn't just mean sheep and cows, but pigs, horses, hens – even llamas! It is important to be aware that this law gives farmers a legal right to shoot a dog which is doing this. A well-trained dog won't chase other animals, and a sensible owner won't let him. But once in a while something can go wrong, which is why that 'stop' whistle training could actually save your dog's life one day. If you haven't yet got the 'stop' perfected, keep away from livestock, and if you have to go along a field edge, use the lead.

Controlling dogs on the road and in public

As the roads get busier, and more of us have dogs, lack of control in traffic and out and about has become an increasing problem. There are now two main laws covering this – the **Road Traffic Act (1988)** and the **Control of Dogs Order (1992)**. Many dog owners will be surprised at the strictness of these laws. For example, the Control of Dogs Order says that any dog in a public place must wear a collar and/or tag with a name and address including postcode of the owner on it (a dog chip identity collar is an acceptable alternative). I suspect a great many country people, especially those who are in the process of working their dogs, will have unwittingly broken this order at some time or another. So, even if you are not planning on going to a public place, always slip your dog's collar and tag in your pocket so that you can pop it on if you have to go on the road or a public footpath. The **Road Traffic Act** is another that people may contravene without realising it. One of its provisions is that dogs travelling in a vehicle should not be a nuisance or in any way distract the driver during a journey – another good reason for having a proper dog travelling box. The Act also makes it an offence to have a dog off the lead on a road, which is only common sense – but be aware that some local authorities have extended this through by-laws to include public areas generally. So letting your dog having a gallop across the park might be breaking the law. If you're worried, just check for signs which will give the by-laws relating to wherever you are.

Mess, damage and nuisance caused by dogs

As public places come under pressure from more and more of us wanting to use them for all kinds of leisure pursuits from skateboarding to dog walking, so the presence of dogs has become more of an issue. There is now some really quite fierce legislation, the **Clean Neighbourhoods and Environment Act 2005**, which provides for fines of up to £1,000 for a range of dog control orders decided and imposed individually by local authorities. Depending on each authority, these include: failing to remove poo; letting the dog off the lead; not putting the dog back on the lead when asked; letting the dog into certain excluded areas; and taking more than a specified number of dogs onto public land. Professional dog walkers need to think about the last of these. Anybody who doesn't take their poo-bags home with them or dispose of them in the designated bins should also remember that £1,000 fine. But the exact rules depend on each local authority. You can either visit your local council's website or go to kcdog.org.uk for more information. Other by-laws also cover nuisance and noisy dogs in the neighbourhood. There is also a law, the **Animals Act 1971**, which makes you liable for damage caused by your dog. It is worth checking your insurance policies (whether pet or household) to make sure you are covered just in case something unexpected happens.

Dog professionals

It is reassuring to know that there are also laws covering the treatment of our dogs when they go into kennels, and the breeding of pups. The **Animal Boarding Establishments Act 1963** provides that boarding kennels must be licensed by the local authority, and of course, they are then inspected regularly. If you are using a new kennels and you have any doubts, you can always ask to look at the licence. Under the **Breeding and Sale of Dogs (Welfare) Act 1999**, licensed breeders have to comply with a number of rules regarding the age of the breeding bitch, how often she has litters and how many litters in all. Breeders are not allowed to let puppy leave them until he is eight weeks old – so do worry about a breeder who is trying to get you to pick up a pup early.

Canine contacts

Armed with this book and the various links listed below to websites in the UK and America, you should have all you need to get started on training your perfect puppy.

PART ONE: The six week survival guide

The Kennel Club, UK is at www.thekennelclub.org.uk, where you will find a huge amount of information, including many links to other useful websites. For the websites of breed clubs of your favourite types of dog, just click on 'breed information centre' at the Kennel Club's website. The website www.discoverdogs.org.uk gives information about the Kennel Club's special dog show to introduce newcomers to the world of dogs.

The American Kennel Club is at www.akc.org, and is also very helpful for information and links across the US, but bear in mind that different states often have different arrangements.

For information about vets in the UK, go to the profession's website at www.bva.co.uk .

For all sorts of dog accessories including beds, indoor kennels, etc. try www.canineconcepts.co.uk or www.petplanet.co.uk and in the USA www.wayfair.com (which also ships internationally).

Good quality car travelling pens can be found at www.lintran.co.uk or www.canineconcepts.co.uk.

One of the leading indoor dog loo brands is the Ugodog indoor dog litter tray; you can also try www.piddleplace.com in the USA.

Microchipping may soon become mandatory in the UK; the charitable Dogs Trust, www.dogstrust.org.uk, sometimes offers free chipping, and www.petlog.org.uk works in association with vets.

PART TWO: How to be a perfect puppy owner

The UK's leading dog charities are www.petlog.org.uk; www.four-paws.org.uk; www.homes4dogs.co.uk; and www.dogpages.org.uk. Also check out www.dog-day.org.uk for details of a charity dog day in aid of the Battersea Dogs Home. In America, one of the main sites is www.animalcharitiesofamerica.org.

The dog walkers' professional body in the UK is the Association of Professional Dog Walkers www.apdw.co.uk; and in America it is the American National Association of Professional Pet Sitters www.petsitters.org.

The most popular breed of dog in both Britain and America is the Labrador retriever. In Britain the relevant website is www.thelabradorretrieverclub.com and in the USA it is the www.thelabradorclub.com.

PART THREE: Puppy from three months to about six months

Among the best places to get training accessories online are www.sportingsaint.co.uk (ships worldwide) and www.traininglines.co.uk.

PART FOUR: 'Big school' training from about six months

Additional training accessories are available from www.questgundogs.co.uk who supply Air Kong training dummies, and see the full Kong range at the website: www.kongcompany.com.

PART FIVE: Your best friend

Crufts Dog Show, the world's most famous dog show is at www.crufts.org.uk.

The Companion Dog Club created for non-pedigree dogs can be found at www.thekennelclub.org.uk/activities/companion-dog-shows.

Organised for non-pedigrees at Crufts, is Scruffts dog show, check out www.crufts.org.uk/scruffts.

For non-pedigree dogs competing in various fields the Activity Register is kept by the Kennel Club, www.thekennelclub.org.uk/registration.

Flyball information is at www.flyball.org.uk.

For Working Trials see the Associated Sheep, Police and Army Dog Society (ASPADS), information at www.workingtrialsworld.co.uk.

Bloodhound Trials information at www.thebloodhoundclub.org.uk.

The Hound Trailing Association at www.houndtrailing.org.uk

Lure-coursing information from the British Sighthound Field Association (www.lurecoursing.org.uk) and in America the sport is run by the American Sighthound Field Association (www.asfa.org.uk).

Greyhound walkers should visit www.greatbritishgreyhoundwalk.org.uk.

Canicross trail running is at www.canicross.org.uk.

British Sleddog Sports Federation at www.sleddogsports.gb.com .

The International Sheep Dog Society (ISDS) is at www.isds.org.uk.

National Search and Rescue Dog Association, www.nsarda.co.uk brings together various regional organisations. In the United States there are several different groups, mainly based in the different states, including the American Rescue Dog Association, www.ardainc.org.

Your dog log

Keeping a full log of your dog's details is really worth doing. Once you have filled all the sections in, I recommend uploading it to your computer. Lots of dog owners like to create their own online page for their dogs, either as part of a family site or even a separate blog. As well as being fun, there are a number of practical reasons for doing this.

• If you ever need someone to come and look after the dog while you are away or out at work, it means all the important information, including emergency numbers, is collected and ready in one place, which saves a lot of time when you are rushing around packing to go on holiday.

• If the dog should ever go missing, you are going to be panicking, so having the numbers of all the dog searchers at your fingertips makes a huge difference. Many dog search organisations have web pages which allow you to create your own 'dog lost' page and poster online, so if you have already gathered together pictures and information, you can have your poster out in minutes.

• If you enter competitions with your dog you will need quite a lot of information for the entry forms and it is always a nuisance searching around repeatedly for the details.

WARNING: Never associate your dog's details with a physical address, and avoid any information which would give dog thieves a clue as to his actual location.

INSERT YOUR DOG'S PHOTOGRAPH:

NAME:

REGISTERED NAME: *for KC registered dogs*

REGISTRATION NUMBER: *as it appears on KC registration document*

BREED:

DOB:

AGE:

GENDER: *male/ neutered male / female / spayed female*

COLOUR:

GENERAL DESCRIPTION:

MICROCHIP DETAILS:

CONTACT DETAILS: *just your mobile number or e-mail, safest not to include your full name*

Useful phone numbers

VET:

DOG WALKER:

DOG WARDEN: *find this through your local authority*

RSPCA: *find your local branch through www.rspca.org.uk*

SEARCH ORGANISATIONS:

www.doglost.co.uk – *an online community which is very helpful and supportive*

www.petlog.org.uk – *mainly linked with microchipped animals, but can be generally helpful*

www.animalsearchuk.co.uk – *free to report and free search elements plus additional support by arrangement, donations encouraged*

www.searchmissingpets.co.uk – *free to report and free search elements plus additional support by arrangement, donations encouraged*

www.nationalpetregister.org – *free long-term register of missing animals*

Dog blog

Use this section online to write about what your dog's been up to! Or you can keep a written record of his achievements and activities.